The United States in 1800

◆◆◆

Henry Adams Revisited

DOUGLAS SOUTHALL FREEMAN LECTURES
1986 ◆ University of Richmond ◆ Richmond, Virginia

The United States in 1800

Henry Adams Revisited

NOBLE E. CUNNINGHAM, JR.

University Press of Virginia
Charlottesville

THE UNIVERSITY PRESS OF VIRGINIA
Copyright © 1988 by the Rector and Visitors
of the University of Virginia

First published 1988

LIBRARY OF CONGRESS
Library of Congress Cataloging-in-Publication Data
Cunningham, Noble E., 1926–
    The United States in 1800 : Henry Adams revisited / Noble E.
Cunningham, Jr.
        p.   cm.—(Douglas Southall Freeman lectures ; 1986)
    Includes index.
    ISBN 0-8139-1182-6
    1. Adams, Henry, 1838–1918. History of the United States during
the administrations of Thomas Jefferson and James Madison.
    2. United States—History—1801–1809. 3. United States—
History—1809–1817. I. Title. II. Series.
E302.1.C86 1988
973′.072024—dc19   88–5514
                                                              CIP

Printed in the United States of America

❖❖❖ *Contents* ❖❖❖

❖❖❖ *Preface* ❖❖❖

Henry Adams (1838–1918), the great-grandson of John Adams, second president of the United States, won his greatest fame as a historian by writing a nine-volume *History of the United States of America during the Administrations of Thomas Jefferson and James Madison*. It was Jefferson who had defeated John Adams in the election of 1800, and Madison was his closest political collaborator. Henry Adams, however, did not begin his *History* with an account of that critical election but with an overview of the United States in 1800, presenting a social and intellectual portrait which was original in concept and bold in execution. Although Adams was disappointed that his work did not gain more fame in his own lifetime, his *History* would come to occupy a high place among the great writings in American history. No part of that work has been more highly praised than his account of the United States in 1800, and it is still widely read today.

The essays presented in this volume are designed to offer a fresh look at Henry Adams's portrait of American society in 1800 and to question whether the scaffolding that Adams erected around that era has aided or impaired historians in getting a clear view of the United States in the time of John Adams and Thomas Jefferson. My intention has been to offer a corrective and not to provide a new historical portrait to replace Adams's account.

The essays were originally delivered as the Douglas Southall Freeman Lectures at the University of Richmond in September 1986. Minor revisions and additions have been made in the texts presented in the three lectures. Freeman, a distinguished historian, journalist, and Pulitzer Prize-winning biographer of Robert E. Lee and George Washington, was a 1904 graduate of the University of Richmond and maintained a close association with the university throughout his life. Having spent the early years of my academic career teaching at the University of Richmond from 1953 to 1964, I take particular pleasure in offering this first of a series of published Freeman Lectures in honor of an outstanding scholar.

I wish to thank the University of Richmond for the gracious invitation to be the visiting Freeman Scholar; I am appreciative of the interested audiences that attended the lectures and the numerous listeners who raised perceptive questions. Among the many persons who made my visit to the Richmond campus most enjoyable, I particularly wish to thank Ernest C. Bolt, Jr., Chairman of the Department of History, for his effective planning for the lecture series and for the hospitality and many courtesies extended. I am also indebted to Harold Woodman of Purdue University for reading a draft of these essays and sharing his insights into American economic history with me.

University of Missouri   Noble E. Cunningham, Jr.
Columbia

The United States in 1800

◆◆◆

Henry Adams Revisited

⋯ Society ⋯

In the summer of 1881 when Henry Adams was in the early stages of writing his history of the United States during the administrations of Thomas Jefferson and James Madison, he arranged with Justin Winsor, the librarian of Harvard College, to loan him books, pamphlets, and volumes of early newspapers from the college library. These were shipped back and forth between Cambridge and Adams's summer home at Beverly Farms, Massachusetts, in a large, strong wooden box with iron handles and a double lock. Adams told Winsor that he wanted to learn all that he could about the social and economic conditions of the country in 1800 and begged him for books that would supply facts, especially if they would correct any of the conclusions that he had already formed. Adams confided to Winsor that "thus far my impression is that America in 1800 was not far from the condition of England under Alfred the Great; that the conservative spirit was intensely strong in the respectable classes, and that there was not only indifference but actual aggressive repression towards innovation; the mental attitude of good society looks to me surprisingly medieval."[1]

Nothing that Adams read during that summer or fall seemed to alter his point of view. As he packed the last box of books to return to the Harvard Library in mid-October, before leaving for Washington to spend the winter, he wrote to Winsor that the sources he had sent him did not contradict his previous conclusions that the world had changed more since 1800 than in the previous thousand years.[2] Though he once again told Winsor he wished to correct this view as much as possible, his basic premise remained largely intact when he published the first two volumes of his *History* in 1889.[3]

---

1. Adams to Winsor, June 6, Sept. 27, 1881, J. C. Levenson, Ernest Samuels, Charles Vandersee, and Viola Hopkins Winner, eds., *The Letters of Henry Adams*, 3 vols. (Cambridge, Mass., 1982), 2:428, 438.
2. Adams to Winsor, Oct. 16, 1881, ibid., 441.
3. Adams's *History of the United of States of America during the First Administration of Thomas Jefferson* was privately printed in 1884; the first trade edition, a corrected and revised

In the first chapter the former assistant professor of medieval history at Harvard wrote that the Saxon farmer of the eighth century enjoyed most of the comforts known to Saxon farmers of the eighteenth century, and he noted that "even in New England the ordinary farmhouse was hardly so well built, so spacious, or so warm as that of a well-to-do contemporary of Charlemagne."[4] He described Americans who were pushing westward as "struggling with difficulties all their own, in an isolation like that of Jutes or Angles in the fifth century" and said that "except in political arrangement, the interior was little more civilized than in 1750."[5] Adams's account of the United States in 1800 may have reflected his reading of Thomas B. Macaulay's *History of England from the Accession of James II,* which stressed the primitive state of England in 1685. In any event, Adams got carried away with his metaphors and flowing words.[6]

For nearly a century, Adams's brilliant mind and powerful pen have awed scholars. Henry Steele Commager called Adams's *History* "the finest piece of historical writing in our literature."[7] A 1980 doctoral dissertation on Adams's *History* pronounced the work "probably the greatest American History written by an American."[8] Only in recent years have historians begun to revise Adams's ac-

---

version of the first printing, was published by Charles Scribner's Sons, New York, in 1889 (Ernest Samuels, *Henry Adams*, 3 vols. [Cambridge, Mass., 1948–64], 2:424–25). No copy of the privately printed text of volume 1 has been found.

4. Henry Adams, *History of the United States of America during the Administrations of Thomas Jefferson and James Madison*, 9 vols. (New York, 1889–91), 1:16–17.

5. Ibid., 1, 5.

6. William H. Jordy, *Henry Adams: Scientific Historian* (1952; rept. New Haven, 1963), 76; Macaulay, *History*, 1:chap. 3.

7. Commager, "Henry Adams," *The Marcus W. Jernegan Essays in American Historiography*, ed. William T. Hutchinson (Chicago, 1937), 195.

8. Ruth Lassow Barolsky, "A Study of Henry Adams' 'History of the United States'" (Ph.D diss., University of Virginia, 1980), iii. William Dusinberre in *Henry Adams: The Myth of Failure* (Charlottesville, Va., 1980) judged the *History* to be Adams's "most impressive work, because he had mastered there both his subject and his artistic form" (p. 2). Although Dusinberre's treatment of the introductory chapters is brief, he lauded the first volume as "the most expertly written" of all the volumes of the *History* (p. 111).

count of the presidencies of Jefferson and Madison.[9] Recent scholarly writings on women, Indians, and various aspects of economic history also have produced findings offering many contradictions to Adams's work. Yet, as a whole, Adams's portrait of American society has gone largely unchallenged. The account, which filled the first six chapters of his history of Jefferson's administration, was reprinted separately in 1955 by Cornell University Press in a paperback edition under the title *The United States in 1800.* Since the publication of the Cornell paperback, that edition has gone through seventeen printings, over 131,000 copies have been sold, and it is still in print.[10] These figures suggest that Adams's account is the most widely read work on the United States in 1800.[11]

Most present-day scholars would probably agree with historian Douglas T. Miller, who has written that "this pioneering effort in social and intellectual history still constitutes one of the most brilliant surveys of any period of American history."[12] They would also widely support the verdict of a leading Adams scholar, J. C. Levenson, that "Adams' six prefatory chapters comprise a mas-

---

9. Merrill D. Peterson in "Henry Adams on Jefferson the President," *Virginia Quarterly Review* 39 (1963): 187–201, reminded historians that Adams's *History* furnished the only comprehensive account and interpretation of Jefferson's administration. Since the publication of Peterson's article considerable scholarly work has appeared, including two volumes on Jefferson as president in Dumas Malone, *Jefferson and His Time,* 6 vols. (Boston, 1948–81); Merrill D. Peterson, *Thomas Jefferson and the New Nation: A Biography* (New York, 1970); Noble E. Cunningham, Jr., *The Process of Government under Jefferson* (Princeton, N.J., 1978); and Robert M. Johnstone, *Jefferson and the Presidency: Leadership in the Young Republic* (Ithaca, N.Y., 1978).

10. Michael R. Romano, Cornell University Press, to the author, Feb. 28, 1986.

11. J. C. Levenson in *The Mind and Art of Henry Adams* (Boston, 1957), p. 149, suggested that most college assignments and popular acquaintance with Adams's *History* usually ended with his six prefatory chapters.

12. Douglas T. Miller, *The Birth of Modern America, 1820–1850* (New York, 1970), 22; see also Merrill D. Peterson, *The Jefferson Image in the American Mind* (New York, 1960), 282; Edward N. Saveth, "Introduction" to *The Education of Henry Adams and Other Selected Writings,* ed. Saveth (New York, 1963), xix.

terpiece of analytic discourse." The republication in 1986 of Adams's complete history of the administrations of Jefferson and Madison in the Library of America series of classic works of American writers attracted considerable public attention. Reviewing the new edition in the *New York Times Book Review*, C. Vann Woodward urged readers to read especially the opening and closing chapters of what he called "this magisterial work"—chapters, he noted, that were "devoted to kinds of history other than the traditional." Writing in the *Washington Post Book World*, Paul C. Nagel called Adams's *History* "the finest historical writing ever done by an American" and said, "Its most famous section is the introduction, a description of the United States in 1800."[13]

That Adams's introductory chapters deserve high recognition as a pioneering effort in social and intellectual history is indisputable, and the account still deserves to be read today. But that his portrait of American society is an accurate one can be seriously questioned. It is not my intention to offer a definitive revision of Adams's account, for to do so requires the reexamination of a vast amount of data available to scholars today that Adams never saw and the use of tools to analyze it that Adams never dreamed of. Because no historian today would rely so heavily on travelers' accounts and other impressionistic evidence as did Adams, the task required is a much larger one than can be attempted here. In these essays I shall focus on areas of Adams's account that need to be questioned and offer some suggestions about conditions in the United States that Adams ignored or neglected.[14]

Richard Hofstadter began his portrait of *America at 1750* by stressing that growth was the outstanding visible fact of mid-eighteenth-century life in Amer-

---

13. Levenson, *The Mind and Art of Henry Adams*, 149; *New York Times Book Review*, July 6, 1986, p. 19; *Washington Post Book World*, July 6, 1986, p. 5.

14. Barolsky, "Henry Adams," an extensive and valuable study of Adams's *History*, gives only brief attention to the introductory chapters. An appendix offers a useful annotated list of reviews of the work in journals and newspapers. Barolsky's summaries of these reviews indicate that the introductory chapters attracted little comment from reviewers.

ica.[15] Growth was no less an outstanding feature of the United States in 1800. Economic development had been disrupted by the Revolution and the period of economic stagnation, even decline, that followed.[16] But economic growth resumed in the 1790s. Meanwhile, the population continued to increase and territorial expansion accelerated. The population of about 1,170,000 in 1750 had passed 5,000,000 by 1800. One indication of the growth of new communities in the United States was the increase in the number of post offices in the decade before 1800. In that ten-year period America's post offices increased from 75 to 903. Instead of noting such growth, Adams emphasized how much smaller the population of five million in the United States was than the fifteen million people in the British Isles or the twenty-seven million in France.[17]

Such comparisons with Europe, combined with a theme of medieval backwardness, caused Adams to fail to appreciate the important demographic changes taking place in the new American nation—the most important of which was the extraordinary growth of the West. Adams belittled this growth by writing that "the entire population, both free and slave, west of the mountains, reached not yet half a million."[18] This hid the fact that by 1800 the West was the most dynamically growing part of the country, both north and south of the Ohio River. The combined population of Kentucky and Tennessee had increased nearly 300 percent in the previous decade. Kentucky alone in 1800 had more people than did five of the original thirteen states.[19] In 1800 Ohio was poised for a population growth so rapid that it would be admitted as a state in 1803 and would have a population of over 200,000 before Jefferson left office.[20]

---

15. Richard Hofstadter, *America at 1750: A Social Portrait* (New York, 1971), 3.

16. John J. McCusker and Russell R. Menard, *The Economy of British America, 1607–1789* (Chapel Hill, N.C., 1985), 367–77.

17. Bureau of the Census, *Historical Statistics of the United States* (Washington, D.C., 1960), 497; Adams, *History*, 1:1.

18. Adams, *History*, 1:3.

19. New Hampshire, Rhode Island, New Jersey, Delaware, and Georgia.

20. Ohio's population in the census of 1810 was 230,760.

Richard Wade in his study of *The Urban Frontier* concluded that the urban pattern of the West had already been established by 1800. With a few exceptions, namely Chicago, Milwaukee, and Indianapolis, every major city in the transmontane region had its beginnings before 1800. The new western cities were still small in 1800—Louisville, for example, had less than 400 inhabitants within the town's official boundaries. But Wade showed that by 1800 a wedge of urbanism had been driven into areas that only two decades earlier had been Indian hunting grounds, bringing "newspapers, schools, libraries, theaters, churches, local governments, and police. Merchandise from Europe and luxuries from the Orient landed at town wharves where they met the produce of nearby farmers waiting shipment down the rivers to New Orleans." Wade pointed out that even more remarkable western development would follow in the next fifteen years—changes that Henry Adams also would acknowledge. But Wade found equally as important the sudden transformation of the western wilderness that took place in the two decades before 1800—something that Adams failed to recognize.[21]

The growth of the West and the accelerated mobility of Americans brought the beginning of a major exodus of people from New England. A comparison of the census figures of 1790 and 1800 shows this clearly. John Bach McMaster printed both these reports in the second volume of his *History of the People of the United States,* published in 1885, pointing out their significance four years before Adams published his revised first volume. Contrary to Adams's image of a static society, the figures also showed that the population of New England had continued to grow, though at a slower rate than other sections of the country. McMaster also reported the Cane Ridge Revival in Kentucky in 1801—an event of considerable social importance. Not surprisingly Adams took no note of the

---

21. Richard C. Wade, *The Urban Frontier: Pioneer Life in Early Pittsburgh, Cincinnati, Lexington, Louisville, and St. Louis* (Chicago, 1964), 17, 35.

beginning of this movement. His image of fifth-century Jutes and Angles left no place for frontier religious revivals.[22]

In characterizing the United States in 1800, Adams said that "experience forced on men's minds the conviction that what had ever been must ever be." "Down to the close of the eighteenth century," he wrote, "no change had occurred in the world which warranted practical men in assuming that great changes were to come." Nothing had occurred by 1800 to warrant the belief that even the material difficulties of America could be removed. He insisted "that radicals as extreme as Thomas Jefferson and Albert Gallatin were contented with avowing no higher aim than that America should reproduce the simpler forms of European republican society without European vices." "Even this," Adams said, "their opponents thought visionary."[23] Adams's emphasis on the strength of the conservative spirit and the repression of innovation made for a pessimistic view. But that such an outlook enveloped most Americans, or even a majority, runs contrary to great deal of evidence. Are we to believe that a generation that within a span of fourteen years witnessed two of the major revolutions in the history of the world—the American and the French revolutions—could be convinced by experience that "what had ever been must ever be"? Adams's view is also in bold contrast to the contemporary observation of François, duc de La Rochefoucauld-Liancourt, who described America as "a country in flux; that which is true today as regards its population, its establishments, its prices, its commerce will not be true six months from now."[24] Adams

---

22. John Bach McMaster, *A History of the People of the United States from the Revolution to the Civil War,* 8 vols. (New York, 1883–1913), 2:576, 578–82; see also John B. Boles, *The Great Revival, 1787–1805: The Origins of the Southern Evangelical Mind* (Lexington, Ky., 1972), 51–69; David T. Bailey, *Shadow on the Church: Southwestern Evangelical Reform and the Issue of Slavery, 1783–1860* (Ithaca, N.Y., 1985), 66–67, 70–71.

23. Adams, *History,* 1:60, 72.

24. Quoted in David J. Brandenburg, "A French Aristocrat Looks at American Farming: La Rochefoucauld-Liancourt's *Voyages dans les Etats-Unis,*" *Agricultural History* 31 (1957): 163;

quoted from Liancourt's travel account a number of times, but he ignored this telling comment.

Adams's characterization surely fit some Americans. Those that it best suited, however, were Federalists, whose party was rejected by the voters in 1800. Jefferson and Gallatin, whom Adams labeled as radicals on the extreme edge of American thinking, were the leaders of the political party that had the support of the majority of the American people. The people who feared change were the ones who lost control of the national government to those who looked forward to an improved and different future, the Jeffersonian Republicans. Joyce Appleby has concluded that the most important element in the ideology of the Jeffersonian Republicans was their "rejection of the past as a repository of wisdom." The Republican victory in 1800 rested, in part, upon the party's projection of a vision of an America that would bring a better tomorrow.[25]

For Jefferson, who was the principal spokesman of the Republican vision, such a promise was not mere campaign rhetoric. Jefferson's optimism for the future of the new republic was firmly rooted in his fundamental belief in the progress of mankind and was nourished by the changes that he had seen in his own lifetime. He observed in Paris in 1789, as he watched the opening scenes of the French Revolution, that few men had had such an opportunity as he to witness in one lifetime "two such revolutions as were never before seen."[26] Earlier, Jefferson had shown himself to be unfailingly optimistic about the future of

---

see also Joyce Appleby, "Commercial Farming and the 'Agrarian Myth' in the Early Republic," *Journal of American History* 68 (1982): 838. Appleby is an exception to the wide acceptance of Adams's account and sees Adams as presenting a distorted view.

25. Joyce Appleby, *Capitalism and a New Social Order: The Republican Vision of the 1790s* (New York, 1984), 49, 78–79.

26. Jefferson to Maria Cosway, July 25, 1789, Julian P. Boyd et al., eds., *The Papers of Thomas Jefferson*, 23 vols. to date (Princeton, N.J., 1950—), 15:305; see also Noble E. Cunningham, Jr., *In Pursuit of Reason: The Life of Thomas Jefferson* (Baton Rouge, La., 1987), 223–24, 239–40.

America, even through the darkest years of the American Revolution. In 1800 he exuded that same confidence, convinced that the new republic could be put on a more republican tack and would continue not only to progress but also to serve as a model for mankind. In his inaugural address in 1801, Jefferson expressed high optimism for the future, seeing the American republic as "the strongest government on earth" and "the world's best hope." While he extravagantly described the United States, whose western border stopped at the Mississippi River, as containing "room enough for our descendants to the thousandth and thousandth generation," his words demonstrated that his confidence in the future was unbounded.[27] That Jefferson was in tune with the majority of Americans was confirmed by the electorate in 1800 and reaffirmed in 1804, when he was reelected to a second term as president with only fourteen electoral votes cast against him.

Henry Adams referred to Jefferson's "sunny and sanguine" temperament, but he failed to recognize the compelling influence of Jefferson's optimistic expectations for the future. In looking at the United States, Adams missed both Jefferson's optimism and the Republican vision of a better tomorrow.[28] Perhaps Adams had read too many New England tracts, sermons, and local newspapers. The books that he borrowed from the library at Harvard no doubt revealed the Federalist mind more clearly than the Republican mind. Indeed, Adams's description of Americans resembled Jefferson's view of many Federalist spokesmen. There is an interesting passage in Jefferson's second inaugural address in which he obliquely addressed such Federalists by way of speaking to the Indians. He warned the aboriginal inhabitants of America against persons who "inculcate a sanctimonious reverence for the customs of their ancestors; that

---

27. Text of inaugural address, March 4, 1801, transcribed from Jefferson's final manuscript copy, Thomas Jefferson Papers, Library of Congress, printed in Noble E. Cunningham, Jr., ed., *The Early Republic, 1789–1828* (New York, 1968), 72–73.

28. Adams, *History*, 1:145; Appleby, *Capitalism and a New Social Order*, 4, 49–50, 79.

9

whatever they did, must be done through all time; that reason is a false guide, and to advance under its counsel . . . is a perilous innovation."[29] In notes that he made on his draft of this address, Jefferson explained that he had "thought it best to say what is directly applied to Indians only, but admits by inference a more general extention."[30] The extension that he had in mind was to the Federalists.[31]

The Federalists feared change so much that they even charged the Republican opposition with fomenting revolution. Congressman John Allen of Connecticut on the floor of the House of Representatives in July 1798, during the debate on the passage of the sedition bill, denounced "the fashionable doctrine of modern times" that preached "a recurrence to first revolutionary principles." "From which may God preserve us," Allen exclaimed. "Do we want another revolution in this country?"[32] The Federalists passed the sedition bill, but that did not suppress the Republican opposition. While the Republicans did not want revolution, they did want change. Missing from Adams's portrait of the United States in 1800 is any recognition of the strong Republican support for change.

The contemporary sources do not dispute Adams's view of the backwardness of the United States in comparison with Europe, especially in the arts and letters and in science and mathematics. But some contemporary commentators were more generous than Adams in noticing advances. Samuel Miller, a New York Presbyterian minister, was one of them. Miller started out to write a sermon in 1801 welcoming the new century and two years later ended up publishing a two-volume work entitled *A Brief Retrospect of the Eighteenth Century.*

---

29. Jefferson, second inaugural address, Mar. 4, 1805, Paul L. Ford, ed., *The Works of Thomas Jefferson*, Federal Edition, 12 vols. (New York, 1904), 10:131–33.

30. Jefferson, notes on a draft for second inaugural, ibid., 127n.

31. In his account of Jefferson's second inaugural, Adams noted Jefferson's allusion but described it as alluding to "New England habits" (Adams, *History*, 3:6–7).

32. *Annals of Congress*, 5th Cong., 2d sess. (July 5, 1798), 2096.

Providing more factual data than Adams and drawing more favorable conclusions from his evidence, Miller saw a taste for the fine arts on the increase in America. He also said that the improvements that had taken place in agriculture during the previous twenty or thirty years were very great, even though they had not kept pace with Europe; and he thought it important that societies for the promotion of agriculture had been formed in all the principal states. He pointed to the establishment of medical schools in the United States as forming "a grand era in our national progress." Medical advances were aided, he noted, by the formation of medical societies in almost every state and by the multiplication of medical publications. The momentum given to the study of medicine in the United States during the last ten years of the eighteenth century, Miller concluded, "deserves to be noticed as very remarkable."[33] While far from uncritical about the advancement of science in the United States, Miller provided a contemporary assessment that Adams might have profited by studying.

The progress in education in the United States—a subject of widespread concern to a generation engaged in creating a republican government—also attracted Miller's attention.[34] The New York clergyman correctly found the establishment of schools further advanced in New England than in the middle and southern states. He also observed that one of the most striking developments of the eighteenth century was the change of opinion regarding the importance, capacity, and dignity of women and the consequent changes in their education. "Female education," he wrote, "has been more an object of attention, and been conducted upon more liberal principles within the last thirty years, in every cultivated part of Europe, and in America, than at any former period." He concluded by saying that at the end of the eighteenth century it was "as rare and

---

33. Samuel Miller, *A Brief Retrospect of the Eighteenth Century*, 2 vols. (New York, 1803), 1:388, 324–25, 2:393.

34. See Frederick Rudolph, ed., *Essays on Education in the Early Republic* (Cambridge, Mass., 1965).

disgraceful for a woman to be ignorant, within certain limits, as at the commencement of it such ignorance was common."[35] Henry Adams, whose great-grandmother was Abigail Adams, could not have been unaware of the advancements in the education of women, but he found no place for it in his social portrait of the United States in 1800.

Abigail Adams, of course, was still exceptional for her generation, but the Revolutionary era ushered in great changes in many aspects of women's lives, including their education. Judith Sargent Murray wrote in 1798 that she expected "to see our young women forming a new era in female history."[36] There can be little question that major alterations were well under way by 1800. Linda Kerber in her study of *Women of the Republic* concluded that great improvements in female education took place between 1790 and 1830.[37] As Kerber's work shows, progress in women's education was not as universal as Miller's enthusiastic report in 1803 implied, but it was a movement of such importance that it must be included in any social portrait of the United States at the beginning of the nineteenth century.

Writing in the 1880s, Henry Adams looked back at 1800 as a time so dissimilar to his own day as to seem closer to the Middle Ages. His own world, transformed by railroads and the rising industrial might of the United States, led Adams to reflect in his autobiography on "the great mechanical energies— coal, iron, steam" that had achieved "a distinct superiority in power over the old industrial elements—agriculture, handwork, and learning."[38] Moreover, he had early embraced Darwinism. Looking at 1800 through those eyes, it was the backwardness of that earlier time that appeared most striking to Adams.

---

35. Miller, *Brief Retrospect*, 2:278–80, 389.

36. Quoted in Linda K. Kerber, *Women of the Republic: Intellect and Ideology in Revolutionary America* (Chapel Hill, N.C., 1980), 189, from Murray, *The Gleaner* (Boston, 1798).

37. Kerber, *Women of the Republic*, 193.

38. Henry Adams, *The Education of Henry Adams: An Autobiography*, introduction by D. W. Brogan (Boston, 1961), 238.

Samuel Miller, writing in 1803, looked back to the beginning of the eighteenth century and sought to show how much American society had changed during the previous century. He cited numerous examples. There were only three or four printers in the American colonies at the beginning of the eighteenth century; by 1800 there were nearly 300 printers in the United States. He estimated that the number of booksellers had increased fiftyfold since the Revolution and thought it remarkable that in 1790 an American edition of the *Encyclopedia Britannica* had been published in Philadelphia.[39] Miller's observations can be supplemented by considerable recent scholarship, which shows a great surge in the publication and distribution of books in post-Revolutionary America.[40] The New York clergyman also noticed the great growth of libraries in America in the late eighteenth century. In contrast to only two public libraries that he could find in the colonies in 1700, Miller reported "many hundreds" in the United States in 1800.[41] Most of these, of course, were not research libraries for scholars. Noah Webster in 1800 complained that there were "not more than three or four tolerable libraries in America, and these are extremely imperfect."[42] But the growth of social and circulating libraries was accelerating by 1800. One modern scholar counted 266 social libraries founded in New England in the decade before 1800.[43]

---

39. Published by Thomas Dobson. Miller, *Brief Retrospect*, 2:386–87.

40. James Gilreath, "American Book Distribution," American Antiquarian Society, *Proceedings* 95 (1985): 538–41.

41. Miller, *Brief Retrospect*, 2:385–86. Something of the progress in building library collections in eighteenth-century America can be seen in H. Trevor Colbourn, *The Lamp of Experience: Whig History and the Intellectual Origins of the American Revolution* (Chapel Hill, N.C., 1965), 199–232.

42. Quoted in Adams, *History*, 1:63.

43. Jesse H. Shera, "Beginnings of Systematic Bibliography in America, 1642–1799," in *Essays Honoring Lawrence C. Wroth* (Portland, Me., 1951), 274; see also Jesse H. Shera, *Foundations of the Public Library: The Origins of the Public Library Movement in New England, 1629–1855* (Chicago, 1949); Cathy N. Davidson, *Revolution and the Word: The Rise of the Novel in America* (New York, 1986), 27.

Miller also saw great progress in higher education. Since the signing of the peace treaty in 1783, seventeen new colleges had been founded in the United States.[44] Adams, on the other hand, pointed to Harvard College as an example of an unchanging society, reporting that on average for the ten years from 1790 to 1800 Harvard annually awarded thirty-nine degrees. Adams contrasted that figure to the ten years before the Revolution, when the annual average was forty-three, and he further noted that a half century earlier in the decade of the 1720s the number of graduates averaged thirty-five per class. The only sign of change Adams saw was a decline in the number of graduates entering the ranks of the clergy.[45]

While recognizing the growth in higher education, Miller still deplored the lack of encouragement to learning. There were "no rich *Fellowships* in our Universities to excite the ambition of students," he wrote. Academic chairs were usually supported by such small salaries that they presented little temptation to scholars, and the state offered few motives for the acquisition of knowledge. Miller attributed these conditions to the commercial spirit of Americans, admitting some justice to the charge that "the *love of gain* peculiarly characterizes the inhabitants of the United States."[46] At the same time, he viewed the establishment of the federal government in 1789 as a major step in the progress of knowledge in America because it promoted the tranquility and confidence required for scholarly pursuits. From 1789 through 1800 literary institutions of various kinds "multiplied with astonishing rapidity," he noted, pointing to the establishment of the Massachusetts Historical Society in 1791, medical schools in New Hampshire and Kentucky in 1798, the Connecticut Academy of Arts and Sciences in 1799, and numerous medical and agricultural societies in nearly every part of the nation.[47]

---

44. Miller, *Brief Retrospect*, 2:381–83.
45. Adams, *History*, 1:77.
46. Miller, *Brief Retrospect*, 2:406–7.
47. Ibid., 1:324, 388, 2:384–85.

It is not necessary to list all the examples given by this New York observer at the beginning of the nineteenth century. He portrayed a record of change and progress that had rapidly increased after the end of the Revolution—a picture often at odds with the images conveyed by Henry Adams, whose perspective from the end of the nineteenth century was clearly influenced by events through which he had lived. Both men were products of their times, though Miller seemed more ready to admit it than did Adams. In the introduction to his book, Miller confessed that men were always "unduly disposed to consider their own times as distinguished, above all others, by remarkable events."[48] Still, Miller may be regarded as a more reliable source than many of the travelers' accounts upon which Adams depended.

We should also note that Miller's account does not support Adams's view of an extensive hostility to innovation. As one living at the time, Miller believed that America was second to none in the ingenuity of individuals, as shown by numerous inventions and improvements in the mechanical arts. He singled out for recognition Thomas Godfrey's quadrant, David Rittenhouse's orrery, machines for manufacturing cards for carding wool by Amos Whittemore, and machinery for making firearms by Eli Whitney.[49] Compared to the development of railroads and the invention of the machinery that produced the industrial revolution in America in Adams's lifetime, these innovations pale, but Miller's enthusiasm for them and his confidence in the innovative nature of his countrymen provides a compelling contemporary refutation of Adams's pessimistic view of attitudes toward change and innovation in America in 1800.

In assessing American attitudes, Adams ignored the American Philosophical Society, which, though hardly representative of the populace as a whole, provided an intellectual leadership of considerable influence and displayed an important strain of thinking supportive of innovation and improvement. Although centered in Philadelphia, the society had a continental and interna-

---

48. Ibid., 1:6.
49. Ibid., 2:394.

tional membership over which Jefferson presided as the society's president from 1797 until 1815. Benjamin Franklin early described the aims of the society as encompassing "all philosophical Experiments that let Light into the Nature of Things, tend to increase the Power of Man over Matter, and multiply the Conveniences or Pleasures of Life," among which he included "New Mechanical Inventions for Saving Labour."[50]

The preface to the first volume of the American Philosophical Society's *Transactions* stressed an emphasis on practical improvements, discouraging "mere speculation" and promising that members would "confine their disquisitions, principally, to such subjects as tend to the improvement of their country, and advancement of its interest and prosperity."[51] At its meeting in December 1800 the society offered prizes ranging from $35 to $150 for such improvements as a new and superior method of "ventilating a ship at sea, without manual labor," developing a cheap fuel for house lamps, and improving the Argand lamp to burn common oil or discovering a cheap and effective method of purifying the oil. The top prize was to be awarded for the best experimental essay on red dyes native to the United States. An endowment enabled the society also to offer a prize of a solid gold plate for the best discovery or most useful improvement relating to navigation or to natural philosophy.[52]

The prominence of Jeffersonians in the ranks of its members made the American Philosophical Society the object of derision by Federalist friends of the Boston-based American Academy of Arts and Sciences, whose members stressed mathematical and astronomical studies.[53] But, as one scholar has re-

50. Franklin, "A Proposal for Promoting Useful Knowledge among the British Plantations in America," Philadelphia, May 14, 1743, reproduced in American Philosophical Society, *Yearbook* (1984), 246–47; Daniel J. Boorstin, *The Lost World of Thomas Jefferson* (1948; rept. Chicago, 1981), 8–12.

51. *Transactions of the American Philosophical Society, Held at Philadelphia, for Promoting Useful Knowledge* 1 (2d ed., 1789): xvii; Boorstin, *Lost World of Jefferson*, 11.

52. American Philosophical Society, *Transactions* 5 (1802): iv–vii.

53. Linda K. Kerber, *Federalists in Dissent: Imagery and Ideology in Jeffersonian America* (Ithaca, N.Y., 1970), 73–79.

cently shown, both the American Academy of Arts and Science and the American Philosophical Society were eager to receive contributions from all the sciences. David Rittenhouse, who succeeded Benjamin Franklin as president of the American Philosophical Society and to whom Franklin had bequeathed his reflecting telescope, made regular observations from his observatory near his Philadelphia home and was elected to the Royal Society of London in 1795.[54] In 1800 the American Philosophical Society was more active and vigorous than the American Academy of Arts and Science, and it represented an important instrument for innovation, improvement, and progress that belongs in any portrait of American society in 1800 on the scale attempted by Adams. Science flourished in eighteenth-century America, though the early nineteenth century brought a period of decline.[55] Surveying American science in the period encompassing the year 1800, John C. Greene wrote in *American Science in the Age of Jefferson*: "In the years from 1780 to 1830 American scientists ceased to be mere purveyors of the raw materials of science to Europe and became junior partners in the Western scientific enterprise."[56]

Some of the data and conclusions advanced by Adams—especially those relating to the economy—lend themselves to testing; others pose insurmountable problems. Adams's survey of the intellect of major regions of America, in particular, was so sweeping and bold, so filled with confident generalizations and striking contrasts, as to defy subjection to such tests of evidence as can be employed to challenge his economic or demographic data. There are, nevertheless, certain limitations of Adams's intellectual portrait that can be pointed out. By focusing on sections, Adams found no place for considering such broad and important questions as the influence of the Enlightenment on American society

---

54. John C. Greene, *American Science in the Age of Jefferson* (Ames, Iowa, 1984), 41, 65, 415.

55. I. Bernard Cohen, *Science and American Society in the First Century of the Republic* (Columbus, Ohio, 1961), 3–9.

56. Greene, *American Science in the Age of Jefferson*, 3.

17

and thought by 1800.[57] Adams's regional investigations were also far from comprehensive. He offered chapters on the intellectual life of New England, the middle states, and the southern states; but of the sixteen states comprising the Union in 1800, only six received more than superficial mention. Adams's South was Virginia and South Carolina. He disposed of North Carolina in a single paragraph and never mentioned Georgia. For Adams the West merited no attention in a survey of the intellect of the nation. Adams obviously knew New England better than any other section, and he treated that region the most fully. Outside New England, however, such an important subject as religion received scant attention.

Even in treating Virginia at some length, Adams gave no hint of the evangelical movement that produced such great changes in Virginia society, as Rhys Isaac has shown in his book *The Transformation of Virginia, 1740–1790*. Adams described the vanishing parish churches, with their doors closed and roofs rotting, but he attributed their demise solely to the loss of state support following the disestablishment of the Anglican church. He did not connect the decline with the evangelical movement that brought plain meetinghouses to supersede the brick edifices of the gentry-dominated Anglican church. Isaac not only associated the decline of the gentry with the spread of evangelicalism but also found a transformation of social customs wrought by the success of the movement. Among such changes, he noted that by 1800 the era of open hospitality of Virginians had passed.[58] I am not maintaining that Adams should have anticipated the findings of recent scholars but suggesting that his portrait of the United States in 1800 is more likely to mislead than to illuminate. It is significant that Rhys Isaac used no medieval metaphors in describing Virginia in the half century before 1800.

---

57. For a recent study of the subject, see Henry F. May, *The Enlightenment in America* (New York, 1976).

58. Rhys Isaac, *The Transformation of Virginia, 1740–1790* (Chapel Hill, N.C., 1982), esp. pp. 302–3, 313–15; Adams, *History*, 1:135–36.

Adam's neglect of the West in his intellectual portrait provides the reader with no basis for questioning his earlier images of fifth-century barbarians taming the wilderness. Yet the records now available, for example, of John Breckinridge's move from Virginia to Kentucky in 1793 offer a striking contrast. Before leaving Virginia, Breckinridge ordered from London over 150 books to take with him and his family to Kentucky. The collection was strong in history and government and included works by Gibbon, Hume, and Locke. In addition, there were fifteen volumes of Rousseau's *Works* and Adam Smith's *Wealth of Nations*. There was also poetry and literature, including ten volumes of Shakespeare and works of Swift and Milton.[59] Obviously Breckinridge realized he would not find well-stocked bookstores in Kentucky, and in taking a library with him, Breckinridge was not a typical western settler. He would later be elected to the United States Senate and serve as attorney general under Jefferson. Still, these facts provide images in sharp contrast to Adams's comparison of western settlers to Jutes and Angles. Nor would the reader of Adams's account suspect that at about the time Breckinridge was moving to Kentucky, subscribers in Ohio were paying ten dollars a share to establish the first library in the Northwest Territory. That library opened at Belpre, near Marietta, in 1796; and the second library in Ohio would open in Cincinnati in 1802.[60]

In surveying the intellectual life of the nation, Adams dismissed newspapers as worthy of little notice. "Of American newspapers there was no end," he wrote, and he thought that the education supposed to have been widely spread by them "was hardly to be distinguished from ignorance." "The student of history," he insisted, "might search forever these storehouses of political ca-

---

59. Lowell H. Harrison, *John Breckinridge: Jeffersonian Republican* (Louisville, Ky., 1969), 33; Richard Beale Davis, *Intellectual Life in Jefferson's Virginia, 1790–1830* (Chapel Hill, N.C., 1964), 82.

60. W. H. Venable, *Beginnings of Literary Culture in the Ohio Valley* (Cincinnati, 1891), 135–39.

lumny for facts meant to instruct the public in any useful object." Adams was contemptuous of the "long columns of political disquisition" that filled many papers, and he was disappointed that he had not found more information in the newspapers on nonpolitical subjects.[61]

Some contemporary opinion of newspapers in 1800 was no more favorable than that of Adams. A writer in the *Monthly Magazine and American Review* in 1799 lamented that "the value of newspaper rhetoric and history . . . , with some few exceptions, is so small as not to amount to any critical denomination."[62] But Pierre Samuel du Pont de Nemours, writing in 1800, presented quite a different assessment, saying that American newspapers disseminated "an enormous amount of information"—"political, physical, philosophic; information on agriculture, the arts, travel, navigation; and also extracts from all the best books in America and Europe." Du Pont also wrote that "in America, a great number of people read the Bible, and all the people read a newspaper," noting that many fathers read aloud to their children while breakfast was being prepared.[63] One thing that all commentators agreed upon was that newspapers were widely diffused and widely read.[64]

Adams made no attempt to provide specific information on the number of newspapers in 1800. Had he done so, an extraordinary growth in the previous decade would have been revealed. From about 100 papers in 1790, the total had doubled to well over 200 in 1800.[65] When Noah Webster started his New York

---

61. Adams, *History*, 1:120.

62. "On American Literature," by Candidus, *Monthly Magazine and American Review* 1 (1799): 342. "Candidus" may have been Charles Brockden Brown, editor of the *Monthly Magazine*; see David Lee Clark, *Charles Brockden Brown: Pioneer Voice of America* (Durham, N.C., 1952), 131–32, 243.

63. Du Pont de Nemours, *National Education in the United States of America*, trans. B. G. Du Pont (Newark, Del., 1923), 4. Du Pont's plan of education was written in 1800 at the request of Jefferson.

64. *Monthly Magazine and American Review* 1 (1799): 342.

65. Donald H. Stewart, *The Opposition Press of the Federalist Period* (Albany, 1969), 16, 651–52.

Minerva in 1793, he wrote in the first issue that newspapers were eagerly sought after and generally diffused. "In no other country on earth," he concluded, "not even in Great-Britain, are Newspapers so generally circulated among the body of the people, as in America."[66] Because Adams was contemptuous of the intellectual content of American newspapers in 1800, he missed the wider cultural significance of both their widespread circulation and their political content.

Adams's focus on high intellectual achievements led him to neglect popular culture. Had he looked for the best-selling work in the United States in 1800, he would have found that the distinction belonged to Mason Locke Weems's brief biography of Washington.[67] Parson Weems, who also was the most active traveling book salesman in America, had begun preparing his short biographical pamphlet six months before Washington's death in December 1799. He was thus ready with a sketch of the late president early in 1800, when demand for everything relating to Washington was high.[68] Few better examples of popular culture can be found than Weems's eighty-page booklet entitled *The Life and Memorable Actions of George Washington*, which attributed Washington's rise to the presidential chair and "the throne in the hearts of 5,000,000 of People" to his great virtues.[69] Weems earlier had predicted that works selling for a quarter of a dollar and calculated to strike popular curiosity would command a large market, especially if they were about men whose courage, abilities, patriotism, and exploits had won the admiration of the America people. Enlivening his narrative of Washington with "*Anecdotes apropos interesting* and *entertaining*," Weems won no critical acclaim for his sketch of the first president.[70] One reviewer de-

---

66. *American Minerva* (New York), Dec. 9, 1793, quoted, ibid., 20.

67. Frank Luther Mott, *Golden Multitudes: The Story of Best Sellers in the United States* (New York, 1947), 305.

68. Weems to Mathew Carey, Jan. 12, 1800, Emily E. F. Skeel, ed., *Mason Locke Weems: His Works and Ways*, 3 vols. (New York, 1929), 2:126.

69. Ibid., 1:2, 2:126.

70. Weems to Carey, Jan. 22, 1797, Jan. 12, 1800, ibid., 2:72, 126; George H. Callcott, *History in the United States, 1800–1860* (Baltimore, 1970), 22.

scribed the pamphlet as a "whimsical production" of "eighty pages of as entertaining and edifying matter as can be found in the annals of fanaticism and
absurdity."[71] But the work would go through twenty-nine editions (some merely
reprintings) by 1825. Its success reflected not only the popularity of Washington
but also the young republic's search for a history. Most intellectuals in 1800,
like Adams later, ignored Weems's work, but since Adams's day scholars have
recognized that the popularity of Weems's *Washington* tells us a great deal about
early American society.[72]

In 1800 Weems also was selling copies of presidential candidate Jefferson's
Notes on the State of Virginia, perhaps the best example of the Enlightenment in
America.[73] The following year found Weems offering his customers engraved
prints containing the portrait of the newly elected president. Published by
Mathew Carey of Philadelphia on the eve of Jefferson's inauguration, the print
presented an image of Jefferson derived from Rembrandt Peale's life portrait
painted in 1800. Some lines from the Declaration of Independence embellished
the portrait. Hundreds of copies of the print were sold, undoubtedly providing
many Americans their first view of what the president for whom they had voted
looked like.[74] The publication of such prints, of which there are a number of
other examples, provides a glimpse into American society in 1800 that Adams's
more limited concept of American culture obscures.

It is not surprising in light of the age in which he lived that Adams did not
include native Indian culture or slave culture in his overview of American society. More recent historians, with a broader cultural perspective, have shown
the continuing dislocation of Indian culture and the evolving slave culture in

---

71. *Monthly Magazine and American Review* 3 (1800): 210, quoted in Skeel, *Weems*, 1:14.
72. Mason L. Weems, *The Life of Washington*, ed. Marcus Cunliffe (Cambridge, Mass.,
1962), xx; Marcus Cunliffe, *George Washington: Man and Monument* (London, 1959), 15–18.
73. See Davis, *Intellectual Life in Jefferson's Virginia*, 79–80.
74. Noble E. Cunningham, Jr., *The Image of Thomas Jefferson in the Public Eye: Portraits
for the People, 1800–1809* (Charlottesville, Va., 1981), 46–50.

eighteenth-century America. Rhys Isaac in *The Transformation of Virginia* pointed out how greatly different the slave communities of Virginia in 1800 were from what they had been in 1740. At the earlier date, about half of the inhabitants of slave quarters had not been born in America. By 1800 all but a very small proportion of Virginia slaves had been born in America.[75] Such studies provide additional support for the argument that the United States in 1800 was quite different from America in 1750.

No one would argue that by 1800 the United States had already attained the American nationality that Adams would define as dominant by 1816. The country in 1800 was only beginning to construct a national history, had not yet created a national literature, and devoted little attention to the fine arts. But American society was characterized by growth and expansion, and considerable momentum for change was evident by 1800. The dominant segment of the population was forward looking and envisioned a better future.

The United States was still a very young nation in 1800, and its place in the world was insecure. Its destiny would be greatly determined by the political culture that had been maturing since independence had been proclaimed. So central was that political culture in the society of the early republic that I have devoted my final essay to the subject, an appreciation of which I regard as essential to understanding the United States in 1800. Before considering that subject it is important to turn to another aspect of society that critically affected the progress of the young American nation—the economy of the United States in 1800.

---

75. Isaac, *Transformation of Virginia*, 306.

··· Economy ···

The economy of the United States in 1800 as described by Henry Adams was both backward and static. He wrote in the first chapter of his *History of the United States of America during the Administrations of Thomas Jefferson and James Madison* that anyone who in the year 1800 ventured to hope for great changes in the coming century could find nothing to silence doubt. "The machinery of production showed no radical difference from that familiar to ages long past," Adams observed. New England had many manufactures but none on a large scale, and the people depended on household industry to feed and cloth themselves. Agriculture everywhere was crude and unproductive; "the backwardness of remote country districts could hardly be exaggerated." Life in the cities was better but hardly inviting. New York City was "so small as to make extravagance difficult." Only Philadelphia, with its paved, partly drained, and lighted streets, its water supplied by wooden pipes, and its model market, evoked much favorable comment from Adams, who conceded that it surpassed any city of its size on either side of the Atlantic for most of the comforts and some of the elegances of life.[1]

Of all parts of the country, Pennsylvania had made the greatest advances, Adams thought, but progress there was no more rapid than the natural increase of population and wealth, while to deal with the needs of America, people's resources and their power over nature had to increase far more rapidly. Adams pictured most of the South as economically depressed, though he did point out the rising demand for cotton and the invention of the cotton gin. He speculated that if any state might hope to flourish rapidly, South Carolina seemed most entitled to expect it, but because of slavery, such a development would only increase social and economic difficulties.[2]

The wealth, property, and financial resources of the United States in 1800, Adams found, were slender and not of a kind easily converted to uses re-

---

1. Adams, *History*, 1:16, 18, 20–22, 27–28.
2. Ibid., 29–39.

quired for rapid development. He saw a disproportion between the physical obstacles to economic growth and the material means for overcoming them. The backwardness, lack of resources, and faint hope for the future that Adams stressed in portraying the United States in 1800 no longer characterized the nation at the end of Madison's administration, Adams concluded in bringing the ninth and final volume of his *History* to a close. The result of the sixteen years under the presidencies of Jefferson and Madison was decisive in the economic development of the Union. "Although population increased more rapidly than was usual in human experience, wealth accumulated still faster. . . . Every serious difficulty which seemed alarming to the people of the Union in 1800," Adams affirmed, "had been removed or had sunk from notice in 1816."[3]

How well is Adams's view of the economic conditions at the beginning of the nineteenth century supported by historical evidence? Was the American economy as backward and stagnant in 1800 as Adams suggested? Was there a surge of economic growth between 1800 and 1816? Evidence available today suggests that these questions must be answered in the negative. Current scholarship in economic history, though offering few definitive answers on a subject for which information is often fragmentary and inadequate, lends little support to Adams's position.

There is uncertainty and disagreement among economic historians as to the rate of economic growth before the 1840s. According to Walt W. Rostow, a great increase in the pace of industrialization in the 1840s brought a "takeoff" into modern economic growth. On the other hand, Paul A. David has argued that the accelerated growth rate of the 1840s was simply a surge characteristic of "long-swings," or growth cycles of fifteen to twenty years, in which growth at an accelerated rate is followed by growth at a declining rate. In the first of three long-swings between the 1790s and the Civil War, the surge of growth covered the years from the early 1790s to about 1806 and was associated with

---

3. Ibid., 1:40, 9:172–73.

the great expansion of foreign trade resulting from the wars of the French Revolution.[4]

This interpretation, based on a far more extensive and sophisticated analysis of available economic data than Henry Adams employed, thus places the year 1800 in the middle of a period of economic growth—not prior to such growth, as Adams pictured it. The careful and extensive study by Douglass C. North also presents persuasive data indicating not that the economy in 1800 was the stagnant one which Adams described but rather that the country was in the middle of a period of sustained economic growth. North concluded that the period from 1793 to 1808 was a time of "unparalleled prosperity," interrupted only in 1797–98 during the undeclared war with France and in 1801–3 during the Peace of Amiens. North's evidence indicated that "this period was a high water mark in individual well-being which was to stand for many years, and laid important foundations for the growth of the economy after 1815."[5]

Working with incomplete statistical data for this early period, economic historians have employed different methods, but the most recent evaluation of relevant studies concludes that the period 1793–1807 was one during which "the economy expanded apace, driven in some measure by the foreign trade factor. Rates of growth of aggregate and per capita real product were high, although probably well below rates achieved later in the nineteenth century."[6]

Available data make it clear that Henry Adams failed to recognize the im-

4. Stuart Bruchey, *Growth of the Modern American Economy* (New York, 1975), esp. pp. 29–31; Paul A. David, "New Light on a Statistical Dark Age: U.S. Real Product Growth before 1840," *American Economic Review* 57 (1967): 294–306; see also Paul A. David, "The Growth of Real Product in the United States before 1840: New Evidence, Controlled Conjectures," *Journal of Economic History* 27 (1967): 151–97.

5. Douglass C. North, *The Economic Growth of the United States, 1790–1860* (New York, 1966), 53.

6. Stanley L. Engerman and Robert E. Gallman, "U.S. Economic Growth, 1783–1860," *Research in Economic History: A Research Annual* 8 (1983): 17–18; see also Thomas S. Berry, *Revised Annual Estimates of American Gross National Product, 1789–1889* (Richmond, 1978).

portant economic growth that took place in the 1790s, particularly that beginning in 1793 as a result of the wars in Europe. Between 1793 and 1801 the
value of exports and the net earning from the carrying trade increased almost
fivefold. The great expansion of exports resulted primarily from a rapid growth
of the re-export trade. In 1792 re-exports accounted for $1 million out of the
$20 million in exports. In 1800 re-exports reached $49 million out of $70 mil-
lion in total exports.[7] Adams gave this development little attention. In discussing the port of Boston, he referred to the extraordinary prosperity caused by
the French wars but dismissed its importance by saying that "Boston had already learned, and was to learn again, how fleeting were the riches that depended on foreign commerce."[8] While it is true that the great prosperity arising
from the United States' trade with both warring sides and their colonies did not
last, much of the wealth accumulated did not disappear, nor was the experience wasted. This wealth and experience would contribute to the economic
growth of the post-1800 years.

In his research on the early American economy, Adams specifically sought
to discover the amount of banking capital in the United States in 1800.[9] The
figure of about $29 million that he provided was accurate, but it appeared to be
insignificant when he wrote that "the entire banking means of the United
States in 1800 would not have answered the stock-jobbing purposes of one
great operator of Wall Street in 1875." By such references Adams failed to con-
vey an accurate sense of the development of banks and of capital formation before 1800. The contrast to his own day was indeed striking. For historical
analysis, however, the reader would have been better served had Adams com-

---

7. North, *Economic Growth*, 25, 221.

8. Adams, *History*, 1:22.

9. Adams to Justin Winsor, Sept. 27, 1881, Levenson et al., *Letters of Henry Adams*,
2:438; Henry Adams, notebook, Henry Adams's library, Massachusetts Historical Society. This
manuscript notebook contains Adams's brief outline for his chapters on the United States in
1800 and notations on sources used; I am indebted to Louis L. Tucker, Director, for supplying
me with a copy of the notebook. See also Jordy, *Adams*, 77 n. 15.

pared the data on capital in 1800 not with his own day but with an earlier stage of American economic development. Had Adams done so, he could have pointed out that when the new government went into operation under the Constitution eleven years earlier in 1789, there were only three banks in the United States, with a total capital of less than $5 million. [10]

In 1800 there were twenty-nine banks, operating in ten states and the District of Columbia, with a total capitalization nearly six times greater than that in 1789. One of the banks that had not existed in 1789—the Bank of the United States, chartered by Congress—had a capital of $10 million. By the time the charter of the Bank of the United States expired in 1811, the number of banks in the United States had tripled from twenty-nine to ninety. [11] Thus the years before 1800 were only the beginning of the growth of banking in the United States. But the economy of the nation in 1800 can be better understood when viewed in terms of growth than when contrasted with the economy of a much different society seventy-five years later in 1875. Furthermore, Adams failed to appreciate the larger context in which the development of banks must be seen—the creation of a money market. There was no money market in America until after the Revolution. Its creation and growth, contemporaneous with the formation of the national government of the United States, was a development of immense importance. Moreover, by 1800 Americans had established connections with the great merchant bankers in Europe; and the factorage system for tobacco, cotton, and other commodities was already in operation, providing credit and financing. [12]

---

10. Adams, *History*, 1:26; Bray Hammond, *Banks and Politics in America from the Revolution to the Civil War* (Princeton, N.J., 1957), 144–45.

11. Hammond, *Banks and Politics*, 144–45.

12. Margaret G. Myers, *The New York Money Market: Origins and Development* (New York, 1931), 3–6; Ralph W. Hidy, *The House of Baring in American Trade and Finance: English Merchant Bankers at Work, 1763–1861* (Cambridge, Mass., 1949), 29–30; Harold D. Woodman, *King Cotton and His Retainers: Financing and Marketing the Cotton Crop of the South, 1800–1925* (Lexington, Ky., 1968), 8–10; see also James A. Henretta, *The Evolution of American Society, 1700–1815: An Interdisciplinary Analysis* (Lexington, Mass., 1973), 202.

Adams also had a restricted view of capital, writing primarily about banking capital and ignoring the warning of Alexander Hamilton, who had cautioned that "it is very difficult to pronounce any thing precise concerning the real extent of the monied capital of a Country." Adams emphasized the lack of capital represented by stocks, writing that "except for a few banks and insurance offices, turnpikes, bridges, canals, and land-companies, neither bonds nor stocks were known." He saw the national debt of about $80 million as contributing nothing to the capital of the country, stressing that it was held abroad or as a permanent investment at home.[13]

Adams failed to recognize what Treasury Secretary Hamilton had explained at length in his "Report on Manufactures": that the securities of the government served as a basis for capital. "It happens," Hamilton wrote, "that there is a species of Capital actually existing within the United States, which relieves from all inquietude on the score of Capital—This is the funded Debt." He elaborated: "Public Funds answer the purpose of Capital, from the estimation in which they are usually held by Monied men; and consequently from the Ease and dispatch with which they can be turned into money. . . . a man possessed of a sum in them can embrace any scheme of business, which offers, with as much confidence as if he were possessed of an equal sum in Coin."[14] Hamilton's Republican opponents did not share his view of the debt as a source of capital, but the treasury secretary's program of funding and a national bank prevailed. Public securities were employed in the capitalization of the Bank of the United States. Of the $10 million capitalization of the bank, $6 million could be subscribed in public securities funding the national debt.[15] Hamilton drew a distinction between an absolute increase of capital or real wealth (which he did

---

13. Hamilton, "Report on Manufactures," Dec. 5, 1791, Harold C. Syrett et al., eds., *The Papers of Alexander Hamilton*, 27 vols. (New York, 1961–87), 10:274; Adams, *History*, 1:27.

14. Hamilton, "Report on Manufactures," Dec. 5, 1791, Syrett et al., *Hamilton Papers*, 10:277.

15. Hammond, *Banks and Politics*, 133.

not claim for a funded debt) and an artificial increase of capital as an instrument of industry and commerce. In the latter sense, the funded debt was similar in nature to bank credit. What Adams ignored in regard to all forms of capital was circulation, or what Hamilton called "the additional motion, which is given to it by new objects of employment." While Adams belittled the national debt held abroad, Hamilton saw it as a useful attraction of foreign capital to the United States to be employed for the development of the country.[16]

Adams thus did not offer a very full assessment of the capital resources of the United States nor provide any sense of the expanding employment of capital. His reference to the limited issuance of stocks and bonds ignored the issuance of some stocks for manufacturing.[17] Such activity was limited but did take place. A woolen manufactory in Hartford, for example, raised operating capital by selling shares of stock, while also being aided by a lottery authorized by the state of Connecticut to raise capital for the purchase of machinery.[18] The Society for Establishing Useful Manufactures issued stock at $100 per share seeking to raise $500,000 for seed capital. Although $625,000 was subscribed, less than half that amount was actually paid.[19] This ambitious venture failed, and, in general, it was difficult to raise capital for manufacturing projects. Nonetheless, Adams's dismissal of stocks and bonds can be misleading. The economy of 1800 takes on a more modern and less medieval appearance when such examples of raising capital are recognized.

In treating American business in 1800 Adams never hinted at the expansion that had taken place in the preceding decade as a result of the enormous increase in the number of company charters granted by state legislatures. Dur-

---

16. Hamilton, "Report on Manufactures," Dec. 5, 1791, Syrett et al., *Hamilton Papers*, 10:274, 276, 281.

17. Adams, *History*, 1:27.

18. Peter Colt to John Chester, July 21, 1791, Syrett et al., *Hamilton Papers*, 9:322.

19. Jacob E. Cooke, *Tench Coxe and the Early Republic* (Chapel Hill, N.C., 1978), 193, 196n.

ing the 1790s, 295 charters were granted. This contrasted to only 33 such charters approved in the decade of the 1780s. Of thirty-three marine and fire insurance companies doing business in 1800, thirty had been established since 1789.[20]

No one would claim that the United States in 1800 was a manufacturing nation. Most of the capital was invested in agriculture and commerce. Household manufactures supplied by far the greater part of all goods made of cotton, wool, and flax. Hamilton's "Report on Manufactures" did not generate much support and produced no major national program to stimulate the growth of manufacturing. In 1800 nearly 83 percent of the labor force was engaged in agriculture.[21] But when Hamilton made his survey of manufacturing in the United States in preparing his famous report submitted to Congress in December 1791, he found more manufactures than Adams saw in looking at the economy of the United States in 1800. Businesses came and went between 1791 and 1800, but because there is no comparable collection of manufacturing data for 1800, Hamilton's data remain the best available information on manufacturing during the decade. They indicate that the state of economic development in the United States at the end of the eighteenth century was much further advanced than Adams's account admits.[22]

In his "Report on Manufactures," Hamilton pointed to an increase in iron-

---

20. Louis M. Hacker, *Alexander Hamilton in the American Tradition* (New York, 1957), 186–87. For economic statistics published in 1806, see Samuel Blodget, *Economica: A Statistical Manual for the United States of America* (Washington, D.C., 1806).

21. Bruchey, *Growth of the Modern American Economy*, 10.

22. The next report similar to Hamilton's to be issued by a secretary of the treasury was Albert Gallatin's report on manufactures, Apr. 17, 1810, communicated to the House of Representatives Apr. 19, 1810, *American State Papers: Documents, Legislative and Executive of the United States*, 38 vols. (Washington, D.C., 1832–61), *Finance*, 2:425–39. An overview of America's manufacturing potential in the 1790s, contrasting sharply with Adams's view, can be found in David J. Jeremy, *Transatlantic Industrial Revolution: The Diffusion of Textile Technologies between Britain and America, 1790–1830s* (Cambridge, Mass., 1981), 8–35.

works and reported that the implements of husbandry were made in great abundance, as were various kinds of edged tools for the use of artisans and mechanics. Most nails and spikes used in this country were made in the United States. The manufacture of firearms was sufficiently advanced, Hamilton indicated, to supply American needs, if adequately encouraged. Coppersmiths and brass founders were numerous. Lead was being produced in Richmond. Sailcloth was manufactured in Boston. "Ships are no where built in greater perfection" than in the United States, Hamilton insisted, and he said that the country's cabinet wares compared favorably to those of Europe. Hamilton also pointed to the manufacture of glass and gunpowder, to tanneries, and to the large quantities of hats made in the different states. He recognized papermaking as a mature industry adequate to national needs and commended the respectable progress that had been made in the specialty of wallpaper. He also mentioned the beginning of the cotton textile industry in Beverly, Massachusetts, and Providence, Rhode Island.[23] Hamilton compared American manufactures to those of Europe and pointed to growth and progress in the United States. Adams contrasted manufacturing in the United States in 1800 with that in America in 1880 and not surprisingly found it backward. Hamilton's perspective, it seems clear, is less likely than Adams's to distort our view of economic conditions in the early republic.

Some of the reports that Hamilton received from throughout the country in response to his efforts to collect information on the state of manufacturing furnish specific and detailed data to support the summary that he presented to Congress. They provide a picture of economic activity in the United States that contrasts sharply with Adams's account. One report to Hamilton described the sailcloth factory in Boston that employed about 200 women and girls and 50 men and was capable of turning out 90 to 100 pieces of duck per week. Another reported the Boston wool and cotton card manufacturer who employed 2,500

---

23. Syrett et al., *Hamilton Papers*, 10:315–34.

persons, including 1,600 women and children, in various stages of production—much of it outside the factory.[24] These reports also tell us something about the early employment of women and children in manufacturing, which Adams never noticed.

From Providence the Treasury Department received information showing that the Rhode Island town was becoming a center of manufacturing activity. A prominent Providence merchant and promoter of manufactures, Moses Brown, reported the beginnings of the cotton textile industry there, together with various other manufactures, including making woolen and linen cloths, rigging, lines, and twine; manufacturing pig and bar iron, slitting it into rods, and rolling it into plates and hoops; and producing shovels, spades, anchors, and other items. Brown also mentioned machines that cut 800 teeth in a minute used in making wool and cotton cards.[25]

The most important development in the Providence area was Samuel Slater's building of the first successful Arkwright mill in the United States at nearby Pawtucket. Slater was not the first to build an Arkwright water frame in America nor the only English mechanic recruited in the 1790s, a time of active American recruiting of talented English managers, machine builders, and skilled workers. But he was the first to demonstrate the profitability of Arkwright technology in America. Slater began construction of the machinery for spinning cotton yarn in 1790 in partnership with Almy and Brown, the largest textile manufacturers in Providence. In 1791 that firm employed twenty-three weavers in their workshop and manufactured more than 12,000 yards of cloth, but in 1796 they abandoned this operation in favor of the putting-out system. Meanwhile, in 1793 Slater moved his machinery for spinning yarn into a specially constructed factory built in partnership with Almy and Brown. The wooden building, erected by skilled, traditional artisans and resembling in form

---

24. Enclosures in Nathaniel Gorham to Hamilton, Oct. 13, 1791, ibid., 9:372, 374.
25. Moses Brown to John Dexter, Oct. 15, 1791, ibid., 440.

an eighteenth-century New England meetinghouse, displayed no outward signs of any drastic break with the past. But the machinery that Slater and his artisans put within the factory's traditional walls was anything but traditional. There Slater built a system of production by which cotton was converted into yarn by specialized machines, linked together by gears, shafts, and ropes and driven by a single source of power—a waterwheel. This was the beginning of the factory system in America, and, of course, it preceded the year 1800. By 1800 the Slater mill employed more than one hundred workers, the bulk of them children. Factory-made yarn became increasingly popular, and from Pawtucket the factory system spread slowly through Rhode Island and neighboring states.[26]

Brooke Hindle has reminded us how much we can be misled by our images of a pastoral early America. One of the reasons that the infant United States was so successful in transferring the technology of the industrial revolution from Europe to America was because early American society was familiar with machines. Adams's rustic farmers do not fit with what Hindle discovered about early American technology. Hindle pointed out that American farmers lived daily with machines—the seed drill, turpentine and whiskey stills, sawmills, gristmills, and the clock. In addition, "a small group of mechanics and artisans worked daily with gears and gear trains, cams, ratchets, escapements, bearings, cylinders, pistons, valves, and cocks—the basic elements of which the new machinery was constructed."[27] These were the mechanics and artisans who built the machinery for Slater's mill.

Leo Marx in his book *The Machine in the Garden* called attention to Tench

---

26. Jeremy, *Transatlantic Industrial Revolution*, 78–79, 84; Barbara M. Tucker, *Samuel Slater and the Origins of the American Textile Industry, 1790–1860* (Ithaca, N.Y., 1984), 50–52, 57–58, 72,78–79, 89; Gary Kulik, "A Factory System of Wood: Cultural and Technological Change in the Building of the First Cotton Mills," in Brooke Hindle, ed., *Material Culture of the Wooden Age* (Tarrytown, N.Y., 1981), 300–316.

27. Brooke Hindle, *Emulation and Invention* (New York, 1981), 3–4.

Coxe as one who recognized "a unique significance to the machine" in America, where land was abundant and labor was scarce and costly. Coxe, who worked under Hamilton in the Treasury Department and contributed to the "Report on Manufactures," extolled watermills, "machines ingeniously constructed," and other labor-saving devices that had been introduced in England. As early as 1787, he had unsuccessfully engaged an agent to steal textile manufacturing technology from England. Through his writings in the decade before 1800, Tench Coxe introduced the industrial revolution into the imagination of Americans.[28]

There was far more economic development in the 1790s than Adams admitted. Eleven Arkwright mills were built during the decade, though only seven of them were in operation in 1800. These seven mills operated about 2,000 spindles and annually spun between 50,000 and 100,000 pounds of cotton into yarn. This was obviously a modest activity, but it represented the acquisition of a new technology and a measure of progress since Slater had constructed his mill at the beginning of the decade. The only recognition that Adams gave to this development was to note in writing about New England that "two or three small mills spun cotton with doubtful success."[29] Adams did not mention the cotton textile factory in Beverly, Massachusetts, which had succeeded in competing with British cloth by specializing in the manufacture of cotton bedticking. The early foundations of heavier industry were also rising elsewhere in America. New Jersey claimed by 1802 to be capable of annually furnishing 5,000 tons of bar iron and 7,000 tons of cast iron and boasted four

---

28. Leo Marx, *The Machine in the Garden: Technology and the Pastoral Ideal in America* (New York, 1964), 153–58; Cooke, *Tench Coxe,* 105; Tench Coxe, *A View of the United States of America, in a Series of Papers, Written at Various Times between the Years 1787 and 1794* (Philadelphia, 1794), 40.

29. Victor S. Clark, *History of Manufactures in the United States, 1607–1860* (Washington, D.C., 1916), 534–35; Adams, *History,* 1:23.

rolling and slitting mills, which on average rolled or slit 200 tons, one-half of which was manufactured into nails.[30]

The United States in 1800 was still a nation of farmers, artisans, and craftsmen—not manufacturers and factory workers. Among craftsmen in New York City were 256 cabinet and chair makers, 26 silversmiths, 72 watchmakers, and 34 upholsterers.[31] I am not suggesting that the United States had entered the industrial age by 1800 but that Adams projected images which distorted the economic changes that were under way, however slowly those changes may have been taking place. Adams's treatment may also have obscured a growing American outlook such as Samuel Miller hinted at in his *Brief Retrospect of the Eighteenth Century*, when he commented on the commercial spirit that prevailed in the United States and the "love of gain" that peculiarly characterized Americans.[32]

Adams wrote about the homespun clothing of Americans and noted that "hats were manufactured by the village hatter."[33] That was true enough, but Adams presented the information in a way that emphasized the rustic dress of American farmers. He gave no hint of a thriving hat industry in the United States seeking to supply the American market and to compete with foreign imports. Something of the extent of this industry was indicated in 1802 when the manufacturers of hats conducted an extensive petitioning campaign urging Congress to provide them greater protection. In a three-month period at the beginning of 1802, petitions flooded Congress from hatters in twenty-seven localities in a well-organized pressure-group campaign that would hardly have

---

30. Clark, *History of Manufactures in the U.S.*, 534–35; E. H. Cameron, *Samuel Slater, Father of American Manufactures* (Portland, Me., 1960), 74; *American State Papers: Finance*, 1:744.

31. Figures are for the period 1800–1804. Rita Susswein Gottesman, *The Arts and Crafts in New York, 1800–1804: Advertisements and News Items from New York City Newspapers* (New York, 1965), v.

32. Miller, *Brief Retrospect*, 2:406–7.

33. Adams, *History*, 1:17.

been expected from Adams's rustic villagers so little different from those of ages long past. Many of the petitions were printed forms with the signatures of the petitioners attached, and they provide images quite different from Adams's picture of the village hatter. Thirty master hatters signed the petition from Dauphin County, Pennsylvania, and each listed beside his name the number of hats manufactured in one year. Individual production ranged from 200 to 1,560, for a total of 17,710 or an average of 590 hats each.[34] That was hardly mass production, but the combined labors of these craftsmen show more extensive nonagricultural economic activity than Adams's account indicates.

One has only to examine the petitions presented to the first Congress that met after Jefferson took office as president in 1801 to observe numerous craftsman engaged in producing a wide variety of goods. Their purpose in petitioning Congress was to seek protection from foreign competition, but in doing so they provided historians with a rich source of reliable evidence displaying a diversity of economic activity little appreciated by Adams. There were petitions from starch manufacturers in Philadelphia; papermakers in Pennsylvania, Delaware, and New Jersey; shoemakers in Lynn, Massachusetts; calico printers in Philadelphia; cordwainers in Wilmington, Delaware; gunpowder manufacturers in Baltimore; and umbrella makers in Philadelphia and vicinity. In addition, there were petitions from manufacturers of stoneware, brushmakers, glassmakers, and printers. During one six-week period while Congress was considering import duties, from two to seven petitions arrived each week from the ever-active hatters.[35] Such data tell us a great deal about economic life in the United States in 1800.

Adams, who seemed to find satisfaction in deriding the limited horizons of

---

34. Cunningham, *Process of Government under Jefferson*, 298; Adams, *History*, 1:16; petition, Feb. 9, 1802, House Records, RG 233, National Archives.

35. Cunningham, *Process of Government under Jefferson*, 306–8; petitions in House Records, RG 233, National Archives.

Americans in 1800, dwelt on the public apathy toward the development of the steamboat. He reported the ridicule that Robert Fulton and others received from their countrymen who regarded their experiments as impractical and visionary schemes. He used that evidence to show the basic conservatism of Americans and pictured them as little inclined to innovation.[36] Yet, Benjamin Henry Latrobe, who also as late as 1803 regarded the steamboat as impractical, reported "a sort of mania" in the United States for "impelling boats by steam-engines."[37] While Latrobe regarded this as an unfortunate diversion from the task of adapting steam power to other purposes, his comments confirm that some Americans were willing to risk the ridicule of their neighbors and the disdain of such a leading member of the American Philosophical Society as Latrobe.

Eli Whitney, the most famous American inventor of the time, had invented the cotton gin in 1793, and by 1800 he was engaged in the manufacture of firearms using a system of interchangeable parts. His method had the enthusiastic support of Jefferson, who had earlier recognized the potential of the idea when it was introduced in France while Jefferson was American minister. Whitney delivered the first 500 muskets made by his new system to the War Department in September 1801. Though Whitney had not originated the idea, he played a major role in popularizing mass-production methods in the United States. Whitney's biographer has written that "this first large-scale American experiment in mass-production methods ultimately held enormous significance for the country. Out of Whitney's 'system' developed the manufacturing techniques that

---

36. Adams, *History*, 1:65–74. In emphasizing the discouragements faced by inventors who sought to apply steam power to water transport, Adams was influenced by Thompson Westcott's *The Life of John Fitch, Inventor of the Steam-Boat* (Philadelphia, 1857), one of the books that he borrowed from the Harvard College Library. Westcott regarded Fitch as "a man faithful amid discouragements, patient under insult, and lofty in purpose against the world's contempt" (p. iii).

37. Quoted in Adams, *History*, 1:68, from the report that Latrobe made for the American Philosophical Society. Latrobe's report, May 20, 1803, is in American Philosophical Society, *Transactions* 6 (1804): 89–98.

formed the basis of the nation's industrial growth." In contrast, Adams wrote that "the machinery of production showed no radical difference from that familiar to ages long past."[38]

Additional evidence contradicting Adams's view of the absence of a spirit of innovation in the young nation can be found in a report from Nathaniel Gorham to Treasury Secretary Hamilton in October 1791 describing the Boston factory of Giles Richards and Company, the largest wool and card manufactory in Massachusetts. Revenue supervisor Gorham spoke glowingly of the innovations introduced in the Richards factory. He said that some of their improvements had excited the attention of Europeans and that models of two of their machines had been purchased by an Englishman. The Richards Company, this observer noted, was "daily profiting by new and happy inventions, which diminish the toil of labor, expedite work, and lessen the price of cards." He described new machinery for making both concave and convex parts "to great perfection, at a very few strokes." A lathe also had been perfected for turning out handles, enabling eight men to produce fifty dozen per day.[39] Such a contemporary commentary challenges Adams's conclusions about the extent of American hostility to innovation and also suggests that the United States in 1800, while far from industrialized, was closer to modern America than to Saxon England.

Recent scholarship offers other evidence to dispute Adams's views of the American economy and the absence of innovation. In a recent book on the merchant community of Philadelphia in the Revolutionary and post-Revolutionary years, Thomas Doerflinger described "an extraordinary efflorescence of mercantile innovation in the Delaware Valley." He found a strong spirit of innovation among Philadelphia merchants and traders, which led them not only into the China trade and the tobacco trade but also into commercial banking, securities

---

38. Jefferson to James Monroe, Nov. 14, 1801, Ford, *Jefferson Works*, 9:312–13; Constance McL. Green, *Eli Whitney and the Birth of American Technology* (Boston, 1956), 118, 131; Adams, *History*, 1:16.

39. Enclosure in Nathaniel Gorham to Hamilton, Oct. 13, 1791, Syrett et al., *Hamilton Papers*, 9:375.

speculation, and textile manufacturing. "Taken together," Doerflinger wrote, "these innovations dramatically advanced the economic sophistication of the port [of Philadelphia] and laid the groundwork for both the upsurge in overseas trade between 1790 and 1812 and the industrialization of the Delaware Valley."[40]

Looking more broadly at early industrialization in America, Thomas C. Cochran saw a society conducive to industrialization and pointed to a "tendency to innovation and ready acceptance of the new in American culture." Where Adams had written disparagingly of American cities, Cochran pointed out that "nowhere else in the world of 1800 were two cities as big as New York and Philadelphia only eighty miles apart and brought into close contact by waterways and level terrain." Cochran found developing in the northeastern United States after 1783 "a culture, including the instruments of government, as well as geographic environment, uniquely stimulating to new economic activity."[41]

Even allowing for the limitations that the materials available to Adams imposed upon his outlook, it is surprising and disturbing that Adams overlooked so much evidence that ran contrary to his pessimistic view of America in 1800. Notice, for example, Jedidiah Morse's *American Gazetteer*, published in 1797, from which the *Boston Directory* for 1800 took its admiring view of Boston. Morse admitted that most Boston streets were irregular and not very convenient, but he described a harbor capacious enough for 500 vessels to ride at anchor in good depth of water. He considered the Long Wharf, which was "covered on the north side with large and commodious stores," as exceeding anything of its kind in the United States.[42]

---

40. Thomas M. Doerflinger, *A Vigorous Spirit of Enterprise: Merchants and Economic Development in Revolutionary Philadelphia* (Chapel Hill, N.C., 1986), 6, 283.

41. Thomas C. Cochran, *Frontiers of Change: Early Industrialization in America* (New York, 1981), 11, 15, 18.

42. *The Boston Directory Containing the Names of the Inhabitants, Their Occupations, Places of Business, and Dwelling-Houses . . . A List of the Stages That Run from Boston . . . A General Description of Boston* (Boston, 1800), 4–5.

In contrast, instead of describing the Boston harbor, Adams focused on the crooked and narrow streets and said that Boston resembled a kind of English market town that was already old-fashioned. He pictured Boston as a sleepy port. On the Exchange "a few merchants had done most of the business of Boston since the peace of 1783," he wrote, "but a mail thrice a week to New York, and an occasional arrival from Europe or the departure of a ship to China, left ample leisure for correspondence and even gossip."[43] On the contrary, the *Boston Directory* for 1800 listed mail stages between New York and Boston six days a week and pointed out that mail leaving New York on Monday at 11 A.M. would arrive in Boston on Thursday at 1 P.M. This is a useful reminder of a very real fact of life in America in 1800. There was no means of land transportation or communication faster than a horse. But there was more frequent and regular communication than Adams indicated, and the exactness with which the mail schedule was published in the *Boston Directory* suggests a more active business community than Adams's leisurely merchants with ample time for letter writing and gossip.[44]

The *Boston Directory* also pointed with pride to the two long bridges across the Charles River. The longest, resting on 180 piers and spanning 3,483 feet, was described as elegant. Both bridges had draws and were lighted at night. The exuberant tone of the *Boston Directory* contrasts to Adams's style of counterpoising progress with the lack of it. Adams concluded in regard to Boston: "Although on all sides increase of ease and comfort was evident, and roads, canals, and new buildings, public and private, were already in course of construction on a scale before unknown, yet in spite of more than a century and a half of incessant industry, intelligent labor, and pinching economy Boston and New England were still poor." Jedidiah Morse, who wrote the account in the

---

43. Adams, *History*, 1:20–21.
44. Samuel Eliot Morison in *The Maritime History of Massachusetts, 1783–1860* (Boston, 1921), 124, described the commercial activity of Boston Harbor in the 1790s as prodigious.

Boston Directory, surveyed the past and saw Boston as making progress. At the beginning of the 1790s only two stages and twelve horses were required on the road between Boston and New Haven, a distance of 164 miles, Morse noted. Now there were twenty carriages and one hundred horses employed. At the opening of the decade only three stages ran through Boston; by 1800 there were twenty-four stages running to and from Boston.[45] In describing Boston in 1800, Adams failed, as he did elsewhere, to appreciate the great changes that took place in the 1790s.

How could Adams be so blind to the evidence of change before 1800 and so enthralled with the record of change after 1800 as to make change the central theme of his summation of the period from 1800 to 1816? One is led to conclude that the literary device of projecting the years of his *History* as an era of dramatic change prevailed over the historian's weighing of evidence. The result was to distort the record of the state of the economy in 1800. The American economy in that year was healthier than Adams depicted it and contained the roots of growth that produced the nation that Adams acclaimed in 1816.

---

45. *Boston Directory* (1800), 6, 7, 146–49; Adams, *History*, 1:21.

··· Political Culture ···

Politically the United States in 1800 was remarkably mature. Americans had found the Articles of Confederation to be inadequate and abandoned that instrument of government in less than eight years, but in little more than a decade after its adoption, the Constitution of the United States proved to be extraordinarily successful. Although strong differences still existed over how some of its provisions were to be interpreted, eleven amendments to the Constitution had answered the objections that had most concerned those who had opposed its ratification. The presidential selection process was still in a state of improvisation, for the electoral plan of the Constitution had never been implemented in accordance to the design of the framers, and the presidential election of 1800 exposed the incompatibility of electoral voting rules with the rise of political parties.[1] When the election resulted in a tie vote between Thomas Jefferson and Aaron Burr, an ominous but brief constitutional crisis ensued. For nearly a week, beginning on February 11, 1801, a deadlocked House of Representatives balloted without either Jefferson or Burr obtaining a majority vote of the states, as required by the Constitution for election. With the term of defeated president John Adams due to expire on March 4, the impasse tested the ability of the new constitutional system to accomplish a peaceful transfer of political power. But on the thirty-sixth ballot on February 17, the deadlock was broken, and Jefferson was elected president.[2] With that crisis weathered, the electoral problem would be corrected in 1804 by the ratification of the Twelfth Amendment, providing for separate balloting for president and vice president. There would not be another amendment added to the Constitution until after the Civil War. Still to come after 1800 were the precedent-setting and constitu-

---

1. Richard P. McCormick, *The Presidential Game: The Origins of American Presidential Politics* (New York, 1982), 3–5.

2. Noble E. Cunningham, Jr., "Election of 1800," in Arthur M. Schlesinger, Jr., and Fred L. Israel, eds., *History of American Presidential Elections, 1789–1968*, 4 vols. (New York, 1971), 1:131–33.

tion-shaping decisions of the Supreme Court under John Marshall, appointed chief justice in the waning days of John Adams's administration. But the acceptance of the Constitution was complete by 1800, and the basic machinery of government instituted to implement that document was firmly in place. The limited size of the central government, its restricted scope, and the rawness of the new capital on the Potomac, with its unfinished buildings and unpaved streets, belied the maturity of the nation's political system.

Missing from Henry Adams's picture of the United States in 1800 was a recognition of that political maturity and any adequate appreciation of the political experiences Americans had had by the time the capital was moved from Philadelphia to Washington in the summer of 1800. Adams may have assumed that his detailed history of the presidential administrations of Jefferson and Madison would give ample attention to political matters; however, in excluding politics from his broad portrait of American society Adams ignored perhaps the most vital element of the emerging culture of the new nation. Adams failed to perceive how important politics in general—not just the political history of presidential administrations—had become in the social fabric of the United States. With the achievement of independence, a national political culture rapidly matured, national political parties formed, and politics became a vital concern in the lives of growing numbers of Americans. The term *political culture* is rather loosely used today, but it conveys a sense of the role of politics in society that Adams missed.

The year 1800 opened with a remarkable manifestation of the political dimensions of American culture. George Washington's death in the waning days of 1799 touched off a wave of public mourning unprecedented in the country and rarely, if ever, equaled again. In the course of the year 1800, hundreds of eulogies were delivered from public platforms and pulpits across the nation, and Washington's enshrinement as the father of his country was complete. He was memorialized in words and pictures. Engraved prints, needlepoint mourning pictures, and pieces of Liverpool pottery presented "Washington in Glory,

America in Tears," and various versions of the apotheosis of Washington appeared.[3] There had never before been anything quite like it in America.

Equally indicative of the pervasiveness of politics in American culture was the contest for the presidency in the election of 1800. Even to Americans today accustomed to presidential election campaigns that seem endless, the length and extent of the presidential election of 1800 appear extraordinary. The flood of campaign literature, newspaper involvement in the election, and party activities were unprecedented. National political parties, which had been nonexistent when Washington took office, had developed so rapidly that the Federalist and the Jeffersonian Republican parties dominated the campaign. With presidential electors being chosen in a majority of states by state legislatures, elections for state assemblies became contests for the presidency. Coming at different times of the year, state elections filled the months of 1800 with almost constant electioneering for and against the candidacies of John Adams and Thomas Jefferson. During the year numerous new newspapers were launched, nearly all of them in support of one or the other of the two political parties. The election demonstrated a widening interest and involvement of people in politics and showed that the voters felt deeply about issues and candidates.

In the same year that George Washington was being immortalized as the founder of the nation and the first president of the Republic, no American was being more vigorously attacked in newspapers, pamphlets, and leaflets and from platforms and pulpits than Thomas Jefferson. The Federalist image of Jefferson as a visionary philosopher unfit for the demands of national leadership was a frequent refrain. South Carolina congressman Robert Goodloe Harper had articulated that image when Jefferson was first put forward as a presidential can-

---

3. Wendy C. Wick, *George Washington, an American Icon: The Eighteenth-Century Graphic Portraits* (Washington, D.C., 1982), 66–73; Davida Tenenbaum Deutsch, "Washington Memorial Prints," *Antiques* 111 (1977): 324–31; Phoebe Lloyd Jacobs, "John James Barralet and the Apotheosis of George Washington," *Winterthur Portfolio* 12 (1977): 115–37; Robert H. McCauley, *Liverpool Transfer Designs on Anglo-American Pottery* (Portland, Me., 1942), 88–93.

didate, writing that he thought the Virginian "fit to be a professor in a College, President of a Philosophical Society, or even Secretary of State; but certainly not the first magistrate of a great nation." He accused Jefferson of "always pursuing certain visionary theories of the closet, which experience constantly contradicts," and of being indecisive when he acted.[4] In the heated rhetoric of the campaign of 1800, that image gave way to one portraying Jefferson as a threat to the stability of the government that Washington had built and as a man who would undermine the very morals of society.

In an address to the voters of Delaware, "A Christian Federalist" exclaimed: "Can serious and reflecting men look about them and doubt, that if Jefferson is elected, and the Jacobins get into authority, that those morals which protect our lives from the knife of the assassin—which guard the chastity of our wives and daughters from seduction and violence—defend our property from plunder and devastation, and shield our religion from contempt and profanation, will not be trampled upon and exploded." The *Gazette of the United States*, the nation's leading Federalist newspaper, asked every American to lay his hand on his heart and ask: "Shall I continue in allegiance to God and a religious President; Or impiously declare for Jefferson—and no God!!!"[5]

On the other side, Jefferson was promoted by his partisans, in the words of one campaign leaflet, as "a man of pure, ardent, and unaffected piety; of sincere and genuine virtue; of an enlightened mind and superior wisdom; the adorer of our God; the patriot of his country; and the friend and benefactor of the whole human race." Voters were reminded that Jefferson had been the author of the Declaration of Independence and were told that his "whole life has

---

4. Robert Goodloe Harper, circular letter to his constituents, Jan. 5, 1797, Noble E. Cunningham, Jr., ed., *Circular Letters of Congressmen to Their Constituents, 1789–1829*, 3 vols. (Chapel Hill, N.C., 1978), 1:62–63. Another South Carolina Federalist congressman, William Loughton Smith, earlier had ridiculed Jefferson as a philosopher in a pamphlet titled *The Politicks and Views of a Certain Party, Displayed* (n.p., 1792); see esp. pp. 28–29.

5. *A Short Address to the Voters of Delaware*, Sept. 21, 1800, pamphlet in Broadsides Collection, Library of Congress; *Gazette of the United States* (Philadelphia), Sept. 10, 1800.

been a comment on its precepts." Throughout the country Jefferson was heralded as "the friend of the people."[6]

Had Henry Adams read more extensively in the partisan literature of this campaign, he would have found a more modern and less medieval society than he described. He would have discovered in some states state party committees with local networks employing modernlike techniques of stirring up interest in elections. He would have found active party workers distributing campaign literature, organizing campaign rallies, and working to get out the vote. Such activities were aided by an extraordinarily active newspaper press. Most of these papers were highly partisan and devoted considerable space to political matters. Adams dismissed newspapers as nearly useless to historians because they gave so much attention to politics.[7] He failed to perceive how much the press revealed about the prominence of politics in American culture.

Writing in the 1880s, disillusioned by the politics of his own day, Adams failed to see in the presidential election of 1800 the depth of involvement of Americans in politics. This engrossment with politics may be better comprehended a century later in a society that accepts the centrality of the presidency in American culture. Close study of the political life of the early republic reveals what an integrative force politics was in American culture and what a dramatic role political campaigns and elections played in the lives of Americans during the early decades of the Republic. The election of 1800 provides evidence that the experiences of presidential politics early became an important part of American culture and that any portrait of American society which does not recognize that development is incomplete.

Had Adams studied the election more closely, he would also have found the

---

6. [John Beckley], *Address to the People of the United States; with an Epitome and Vindication of the Public Life and Character of Thomas Jefferson* (Philadelphia, 1800), 32; *To the People of New Jersey*, signed by Joseph Bloomfield, chairman, Sept. 30, 1800, broadside, Historical Society of Pennsylvania; *Maryland Gazette* (Annapolis), Apr. 3, 1800.

7. Cunningham, "Election of 1800," in Schlesinger and Israel, *History of American Presidential Elections*, 1:106–9, 114–15, 125; Adams, *History*, 1:120.

momentum for change that he thought so lacking in American society. The attitudes repressive to change, which Adams saw as dominant, clearly existed within the ranks of the Federalists. But if any common denominator characterized the Republicans, it was their vision of a changed and better tomorrow.[8] Patterns of political allegiance were intricate, and no single pattern explains political behavior in 1800. But one close student of partisan allegiance found that the single variable that correlated more closely than any other with voting behavior in 1800 was the rate of population growth. Federalists were more likely to be strongest in areas with the smallest growth rate; Republicans more often were dominant in more dynamic, growing areas.[9] Campaign literature, too, reflected the Federalist resistance to change and the Republican hope for a different future. Federalists praised the "present prosperous situation" of the nation and expected the voters to "value the blessings of a good government too well to risque a change."[10] On the other hand, Republicans asked, "Is it not high time for a change?" The Philadelphia *Aurora*, the leading Jeffersonian newspaper in 1800, printed a version of the Republican platform, using two parallel columns to list "Things As They Have Been" under the Federalists and "Things As They Will Be" under the Republicans.[11] Only by neglecting the political contest of 1800 could Adams posit a static society little changed from times long past.

---

8. Appleby, *Capitalism and a New Social Order*, 48–50, 79.

9. David Hackett Fischer, *The Revolution of American Conservatism: The Federalist Party in the Era of Jeffersonian Democracy* (New York, 1965), 201, 215–17.

10. *An Address to the Citizens of North Carolina on the Subject of the Approaching Elections*, July 1800, signed "A North Carolina Planter" [n.p., 1800], 6, pamphlet, University of North Carolina Library; *An Address to the Voters for Electors of President and Vice President of the United States, in the State of Virginia*, Richmond, May 26, 1800, signed by William Austin, broadside, Library of Congress.

11. *Republican Meeting . . . of Republican Citizens of the County of Burlington . . . 20th September, 1800 . . . Address* (Mount Holly, N.J., 1800), 16, pamphlet, New York Public Library; *Aurora* (Philadelphia), Oct. 14, 1800.

50

Adams quoted Jefferson's famous reflection that the election of 1800 was "as real a revolution in the principles of our government as that of 1776 was in its form." Adams stopped at this point and did not include the remainder of the sentence, in which Jefferson wrote that the revolution of 1800 was "not effected indeed by the sword" as that of 1776 "but by the rational and peaceable instrument of reform, the suffrage of the people." That was a telling omission, for it denied the Jeffersonian revolution its democratic base in the suffrage of the people and allowed Adams to write that "Jefferson and his Southern friends took power as republicans opposed to monarchists, not as democrats opposed to oligarchy." "His Northern followers were in the main democrats," Adams indicated; but Jefferson and "most of his Southern partisans claimed to be republicans, opposed by secret monarchists."[12]

Adams, who had earlier written a biography of John Randolph, emphasized a conflict between southern republicanism and northern democracy, which he saw in Jefferson's writings; and he derided Jefferson's inaugural commitment promising "absolute acquiescence in the decisions of the majority."[13] Adams, who had been twenty-three years old when the Civil War began, detested slavery and entitled the chapter on the outbreak of the Civil War in his autobiography "Treason." To him Jeffersonian democracy was Virginia republicanism, or "the Virginia school." In commenting on Jefferson's inaugural declaration, Adams wrote, "No principle was so thoroughly entwined in the roots of Virginia republicanism as that which affirmed the worthlessness of decisions made by a majority of the United States, either as a nation or a confederacy, in matters which concerned the exercise of doubtful powers." As proof, he cited the Kentucky and Virginia Resolutions of 1798. Adams did not recognize Jefferson's inaugural declaration to be a reaffirmation of a democratic

---

12. Jefferson to Spencer Roane, Sept. 6, 1819, Ford, *Jefferson Works*, 12:136; Adams, *History*, 1:208–9.

13. Adams, *History*, 1:205; Jefferson, inaugural address, Mar. 4, 1801, Cunningham, *Early Republic*, 74.

faith that Jefferson had long avowed. More than a decade earlier, Jefferson had eloquently and publicly affirmed the same creed in an address presented on the eve of his joining Washington's administration as secretary of state in 1790. Extolling the "blessings of self-government," Jefferson had then stated his belief that "the will of the majority, the Natural law of every society, is the only sure guardian of the rights of man." And he urged his fellow-citizens to bow to that will, "even in it's deviations, for it soon returns again to the right way."[14]

Neither then nor in his inaugural speech did Jefferson address the question of how the sense of the majority was to be taken. He never envisioned that sense being best expressed in an all-powerful central government; but his faith in the principle of majority rule was at the heart of the basic political beliefs that constituted Jeffersonian democracy. His reaffirmation of that principle in the campaign of 1800 and at his inauguration as president gave momentum to expanding its application and to the transformation of republicanism into a broadening democracy. Adams noted that Jefferson "believed that his task in the world was to establish a democratic republic," and he recognized that "Jefferson aspired beyond the ambition of a nationality, and embraced in his view the whole future of man." But Adams gave emphasis to the tradition of states' rights that claimed heritage from Jefferson to the neglect of the tradition of democratic rights with which Jefferson was even more closely identified in 1800. In the end, Adams emphasized the complexity of Jefferson. "The contradictions in Jefferson's character have always rendered it a fascinating study," he wrote. "A few broad strokes of the brush would paint the portraits of all the early Presidents with this exception . . . but Jefferson could be painted only touch by touch, with a fine pencil, and the perfection of the likeness depended upon the shifting and uncertain flicker of its semi-transparent shadows."[15]

---

14. Adams, *Education*, 44–51, 98; Adams, *History*, 1:143, 205, 253; Jefferson, address to the citizens of Albemarle County, Virginia, Feb. 12, 1790, Boyd, *Jefferson Papers*, 16:179, published in *Gazette of the United States* (New York), Mar. 24, 1790.

15. Adams, *History*, 1:146, 179, 277.

Still, Adams failed to give adequate recognition to the impact of Jefferson's ideals on American political culture as it had matured by 1800.

Whether the term *revolution* that Jefferson used to describe the election of 1800 is employed or not, that election was one of the critical elections in American history, marking important changes in the political system of the new nation. Along with a broadening popular participation in politics, it demonstrated the ability of the government under the Constitution to transfer national power from one political party to another. John Adams's taking office as president four years earlier had been largely a succession. After being vice president under Washington, Adams advanced to the presidential chair. To underscore the continuity, Adams had retained all of his predecessor's cabinet. When Jefferson assumed the presidential office, a complete change in the executive branch took place for the first time in American history. A similar transition also occurred in Congress, as Republican majorities in both houses replaced the Federalist majorities that had controlled Congress under President Adams. After the tie between Jefferson and Burr in the electoral vote, that this transfer of political power was accomplished peacefully demonstrated the maturity of the nation's political system and gave unprecedented meaning to the election that dominated the year 1800. Moreover, the defeated Federalist party continued to contest Republican power through the election process, copying in many localities Republican campaign methods and party mechanisms. Such party competition fostered popular participation in politics and the expansion of political democracy.[16]

Our understanding of the political culture of America in 1800 can be enhanced by studying parties and elections. It can also be broadened by examining the relationships between the people and their elected representatives. In a society where politics operated on local, state, and national levels, there was much variation and fluctuating interest, depending upon specific issues being

---

16. Fischer, *Revolution of American Conservatism*, xi-xix.

contested or individual candidates competing for office.[17] But on every level there was an involvement in politics that Henry Adams did not adequately appreciate. Adams's study provided little sense of the relationships between ordinary people and their elected representatives. He ignored some of the most revealing manifestations of the involvement of people in national politics. One of these was the petitioning process, a practice which many historians besides Adams also have neglected.

To a degree difficult to appreciate today, the right to petition the national government was a vital part of the political process in the early republic. On matters that most Americans today would write to their representatives or senators, Americans in 1800 petitioned Congress directly. They also wrote to their congressmen as well and, indeed, commonly directed their petitions to a member to introduce on the floor of Congress. But unlike their letters to members, petitions put their concerns directly before the legislative body. In fact, petitions accounted for much of the work of the early congresses. Most standing committees in the formative years owed their existence in large part to the business of handling petitions. These petitions were so numerous and today fill so many boxes in the National Archives that it is difficult to understand how the idea of distance from government and apathy toward what was happening in Washington could become so widely accepted.[18]

Some foreign visitors to America in Jefferson's day sensed the extent of popular involvement in politics, among them Isaac Weld, Jr., an English traveler in the later 1790s. We know from the notebooks that Adams kept on his re-

---

17. See J. R. Pole, *Political Representation in England and the Origins of the American Republic* (Berkeley, Calif., 1971), 541–64.

18. On petitions, see Cunningham, *Process of Government under Jefferson*, 294–315. James Sterling Young in *The Washington Community, 1800–1828* (New York, 1966) argued that the national government in Washington at the beginning of the nineteenth century was "at a distance and out of sight" and its activities were of not much interest to most Americans (see esp. pp. 27–37).

search for his *History* that he used Weld's travel account in forming his picture of American society in 1800. He cited Weld in reporting the deplorable conditions in American inns, which rarely escaped the censure of foreign and American travelers alike. But Adams would have revealed something of greater significance had he quoted Weld's comments on the involvement of Americans in politics. "The Americans," Weld observed, " . . . are for ever cavilling at some of the public measures; something or other is always wrong, and they never appear perfectly satisfied. If any great measure is before congress for discussion, seemingly distrustful of the abilities or the integrity of the men they have elected, they meet together in their towns or districts, canvass the matter themselves, and then send forward instructions to their representatives how to act." Weld also noted after a stop in a crowded tavern that it was scarcely possible for a dozen Americans to sit together without quarreling about politics.[19] This English traveler saw something that Adams omitted from his portrait of American society. Americans were very much a political people.

Weld's observations that Americans were debating political issues at taverns and gathering in public meetings to send instructions to their elected representatives are supported by the correspondence files of members of Congress. Public interest in national politics is also confirmed by the attention that the press gave to national issues. That included the extensive reporting of congressional debates in the newspapers and the public airing of national political issues in popular pamphlets. Congressional debates were more fully reported in the newspapers in 1800 than they are today. Many congressmen also helped to keep their constituents informed by regularly reporting to them in printed circular letters discussing the business of each session of Congress.[20]

---

19. Notebook in Henry Adams's library, Massachusetts Historical Society; Isaac Weld, Jr., *Travels through the States of North America, and the Provinces of Upper and Lower Canada, during the Years 1795, 1796, and 1797*, 2 vols. (3d ed., London, 1800), 1:124–25, 102.
20. Cunningham, *Circular Letters of Congressmen to Their Constituents*, 1:xv-xlv.

The proceedings of the government in Washington, despite the physical isolation of the city in 1800, were neither out of sight nor out of mind. Americans might not have been much interested in the fine arts, as many Americans as well as foreign observers noticed, but they were interested in politics. And in a world in which monarchy was the dominant form of government, the people of the United States in 1800 were creating a new political society. We cannot isolate politics from a social history of the United States. Politics was the essence of the new republican society. Pointing to the public orientation of American thought in the post-Revolutionary era, Ralph Ketcham has noted the strong political theme that dominated speculations on American character and concluded that "the most creative, influential considerations of the nation's character were one way or another proposals for law and public policy."[21]

The decline of deference in American society was noticeable before 1800. English traveler Weld believed that many common people in America went out of their way to be rude to travelers dressed as gentlemen, just to demonstrate the equality of American society. A generation later Alexis de Tocqueville would find equality the most important condition of democracy in America. The United States in 1800 was far more alien to the Middle Ages than to the age of Jackson—the age that Henry Adams was born into in 1838. Indeed, the changes that we have come to associate with Jacksonian democracy were already underway in 1800. Before that date Vermont had become the first American state formally to divorce property holding or tax paying from the right to vote, extending the suffrage to all adult males who would take the freeman's oath. As other states shifted from a property-holding to a tax-paying requirement for voting, a very broad electorate was created.[22] The growth of political

21. Ralph Ketcham, *From Colony to Country: The Revolution in American Thought, 1750–1820* (New York, 1974), 260.

22. Weld, *Travels*, 1:30; Chilton Williamson, *American Suffrage: From Property to Democracy, 1760–1860* (Princeton, N.J., 1960), 98, 135–36.

parties also stimulated popular participation in politics. Although the initiative for early party organization commonly came from party leaders, once the leaders began organizing mass meetings and mobilizing the voters to win elections, as the Jeffersonians were doing by 1800, the involvement of large numbers of people in party affairs led not only to increased popular participation in politics but also to a gradual democratization of the conduct of party affairs.[23] The winds of change were rising in the America of 1800 that Adams thought so static.

In emphasizing Jefferson's Virginia republicanism and in presenting a portrait of American intellectual life in 1800 in separate chapters on New England, the middle states, and the South, Adams gave more emphasis to sectionalism than may be warranted. Sectional distinctiveness and differences abounded in 1800, but the Constitution had struck a political compromise and a balance that had not yet been seriously questioned. Jefferson's Kentucky Resolutions and Madison's Virginia Resolutions challenging the constitutionality of the alien and sedition acts, while expounding a states' rights interpretation of the Constitution, were advanced in the defense of civil liberties, not in the pursuit of sectional interests. Moreover, the resolutions did not provoke a sectional response.

Sectional associations were indeed evident in political parties, and appeals to sectional interests and prejudices appeared in partisan campaign literature.[24] The Federalists were always strongest in New England, and the Jeffersonian Republicans were strongest in the South and the West. But the middle Atlantic states were closely divided, and the most important political alignment contrib-

---

23. Noble E. Cunningham, Jr., *The Jeffersonian Republicans: The Formation of Party Organization, 1789–1801* (Chapel Hill, N.C., 1957), 251–55, 258–61.

24. See, for example, *A Candid Address to the Freemen of the State of Rhode-Island on the Subject of the Approaching Election, from a Number of Their Fellow Citizens* (Providence, [1800]), broadside, John Carter Brown Library, reprinted in Cunningham, "Election of 1800," in Schlesinger and Israel, *History of American Presidential Elections*, 1:140–43.

uting to the Jeffersonian political success was the alliance of New York and Virginia Republicans. The most exhaustive study of roll-call voting in the early congresses shows that sectional influences in voting declined in the decade of the 1790s. While regional considerations had been strong in the first two congresses, party had surpassed region as a major influence by the beginning of the Third Congress. The decline in regional influence continued throughout the decade. By 1800 the role of sectionalism had nearly disappeared as a determinant of congressional voting.[25]

That party was a stronger force than sectionalism was also illustrated in the residence patterns of congressmen in the boardinghouses of Washington. In that new city, where most members of Congress lived only a few months out of each year and came without their families, congressmen shared rooms with colleagues, often from their own or a neighboring state. When one examines the congressional rosters that listed members' local addresses by boardinghouses, the most striking thing that first meets the eye is the regional character of the groups residing in the different houses. But a closer analysis reveals an even more important factor at work—that of party. The congressional directory for the first session of the Seventh Congress—the first Congress to meet during Jefferson's presidency—listed eleven major boardinghouses containing groups of from six to twelve members. Seven of these houses were Republican, and four were Federalist. Not one of them housed members of opposite parties. When regional affinity and party identification did not coincide, region yielded to party. A southerner found boarding with a group of New England Federalists will be found to be a Federalist. A lone New Englander living with a group of southern Republicans will be found to be a Republican. Most boardinghouses contained a majority of members from one section, but the residents of only two

---

25. John F. Hoadley, *Origins of American Political Parties, 1789–1803* (Lexington, Ky., 1986), 177–79.

of the eleven boardinghouses were exclusively from a single region.[26]

The dominance of party revealed by the living patterns shown in congressional rosters is supported by the observations of contemporary commentators. One Washington visitor wrote in 1803 that "no Tavern or boardinghouse contains two members of opposite sentiments."[27] While section yielded to party in such residence decisions, party also at times incited sectionalism. Jefferson's election and the subsequent purchase of Louisiana provoked a strident sectional response from some New England Federalists. Timothy Pickering and a few disgruntled New Englanders even plotted secession. But the more significant fact is that Pickering and his friends found so little support for their scheme.[28] Before the end of his first term, Jefferson and his administration enjoyed substantial support in all parts of the country, including New England. Interests broader than those of section prevailed.

The 1800 slavery was less a basis for sectionalism than it would become two decades later when the controversy over the admission of Missouri into the Union rocked the country and left even the optimistic Jefferson shaken and fearful for the future of the Union. In 1800 Jefferson was still confident that the younger generation would deal with the problem of slavery that his generation had failed to face up to, though he reacted to the news of Gabriel's abortive slave uprising near Richmond in 1800 with uncharacteristic gloom. "We are truly to be pitied," he confided to Benjamin Rush. Henry Adams had little to say

26. *List of Members of the Senate and House of Representatives, with Their Places of Abode* [December 1801], Rare Book Division, Library of Congress; Cunningham, *Process of Government under Jefferson,* 283–84.

27. Benjamin G. Orr to John Steele, Feb. 13, 1803, Henry W. Wagstaff, ed., *The Papers of John Steele,* 2 vols. (Raleigh, N.C., 1924), 1:361. For other examples, see Cunningham, *Process of Government under Jefferson,* 284–85.

28. Gerard H. Clarfield, *Timothy Pickering and the American Republic* (Pittsburgh, 1980), 225–28.

about slavery in his survey of the United States in 1800 except to picture it as depressing the South. Had he examined the institution more closely, he might have noted that slavery was still only partly on its way to extinction outside the South. Only two states—Massachusetts and Vermont—reported no slaves in the census of 1800. New York, which did not provide for gradual emancipation of slaves until 1799, reported more than 20,000 slaves in 1800. New Jersey, which did not follow New York's example of gradual emancipation until 1804, had over 12,000 slaves in 1800.[29] In neither North nor South was there an urgency to deal with the ending of slavery.[30] Jefferson had sought to prod his fellow Virginians toward adopting some plan of gradual emancipation, but his voice had been a lonely one.

Among writers concerned about challenges to the young nation, there was far more urgency voiced in regard to the education of citizens for a republican society than with respect to ending slavery. Those concerned about education directed much thought toward some national system of education.[31] President Washington had proposed the establishment of national university, and Jefferson would renew the recommendation after he became president.[32] The fact that Congress never acted on their proposals suggests that there were limits to the nationalism of the early republic, but this was an expression of developing nationality that Adams might have noted.

Much has been written on the early republic since Adams's time. A histo-

---

29. Jefferson to Rush, Sept. 23, 1800, [Merrill D. Peterson, ed.], *Thomas Jefferson Writings* (New York, 1984), 1082; Adams, *History*, 1:33–35, 135; *Return of the Whole Number of Persons within the Several Districts of the United States: According to "An Act providing for the Second Census or Enumeration of the Inhabitants of the United States"* (Washington, D.C., 1802), 46–48, 89; *Literary Magazine and American Register* 1 (1804): 474.

30. See Donald Robinson, *Slavery in the Structure of American Politics, 1765–1820* (New York, 1979), 248–50, 424–27.

31. See Rudolph, *Essays on Education in the Early Republic*, ix-xxi.

32. Fred L. Israel, ed., *The State of the Union Messages of the Presidents, 1790–1966*, 3 vols. (New York, 1967), 1:35, 88.

rian writing at the end of the nineteenth century cannot be faulted for not anticipating the discoveries and new insights that subsequent scholarship has provided. At the same time, we should not be beguiled by Adams's intellect and the artistry of his *History* into accepting his assessment of American society without questioning its adequacy for portraying the United States in 1800. It can be argued that Adams failed to demonstrate an adequate appreciation of the political culture of the United States and to sense the full dimensions of Jefferson's electoral victory in 1800. That election brought into office not the Virginia Republican that Adams was prone to see but a party leader who had national support and who articulated a political vision widely shared. In manifesting a faith in the people and a confidence in the will of the majority, Jefferson brought to the presidential office a democratic faith unmatched by either of his predecessors in that high office. In failing to appreciate fully the impact of the political consequences of the election of 1800, Adams missed an opportunity to provide a deeper understanding of American society in 1800.

··· Epilogue ···

If, as I have argued in these essays, Adams misjudged the state of the nation in 1800, how can this be explained? No historian of his day was more scientific in his historical method. Adams worked from original sources, and he evaluated their usefulness and objectivity. In using travelers' accounts, for example, he assessed their biases and outlooks and frequently alerted the reader to these considerations.[1] But Adams undertook his research on the year 1800 without adequate study of the period before 1800. Except for his biographies of John Randolph and Albert Gallatin, he had not delved deeply into the sources for the years preceding 1800, and he would never undertake any research on the 1780s and 1790s comparable to his investigation of the two decades after 1800. Adams also suffered from the limitations of the scholarship of his time. The newly developing discipline of political science, for example, was only beginning to study political parties. Even more important than such scholarly limitations was the impact of the age in which he lived. Adams was the product of his time, a world so profoundly different from 1800 as to make that earlier age seem closer to Charlemagne than to Charles Darwin. Finally, and perhaps most important in explaining Adams's treatment of American society in 1800, was his literary craftsmanship. Adams was a writer who devoted much effort to perfecting his narrative. Therein lies much of the continuing appeal of his work and no small measure of the problem with his account as a work of history.[2]

Why Adams shaped the images of 1800 the way he did becomes clearer when one reads the concluding chapters of his monumental work. In the final volume of his account of the administration of President Madison, Adams looked at the United States at the end of 1816 and found a completely different country than in 1800. American nationality had taken shape by 1816. "Ameri-

---

1. William R. Taylor, "Historical Bifocals on the Year 1800," *New England Quarterly* 23 (1950): 176–77.

2. In recent years Adams's *History* has attracted more attention from literary scholars than from historians. See Barolsky, "Henry Adams," 3–6, 397–406.

can character was formed, if not fixed," he wrote, while concluding that "every serious difficulty which seemed alarming to the people of the Union in 1800 had been removed or sunk from notice in 1816."[3] Adams's contrast between a people in 1800 who had not yet freed themselves from the Middle Ages and a people in 1816 ready to march into modern times—Adams's own age—gave remarkable literary artistry to his narrative. But it did injustice to history by compressing into a sixteen-year period developments that had been shaping for some time— at least since independence from Great Britain, and in many respects for a much longer period. Because his study of the years before 1800 was deficient, Adams was unprepared to question his view of the United States in 1800 or to challenge the grand organizing theme he built upon it.

Adams gave some hints of his theme in the first volume. As J. C. Levenson pointed out in *The Mind and Art of Henry Adams*, Adams evoked images of Edward Gibbon musing upon the decline and fall of the Roman Empire when he described the new capital in Washington in 1800.[4] Adams's theme would not be decline and fall but a rising nation, still unsure of its identity in 1800 but destined to achieve nationality by 1816. In writing of the new city rising on the banks of the Potomac in 1800, he emphasized "the contrast between the immensity of the task and the paucity of means," and he pondered the consequences of Congress's doling out funds "with so sparing a hand, that their Capitol threatened to crumble in pieces and crush Senate and House under the ruins, long before the building was complete." He continued: "A government capable of sketching a magnificent plan, and willing to give only a half-hearted pledge of its fulfillment; a people eager to advertise a vast undertaking beyond their present, which when completed would become an object of jealousy and fear,—this was the impression made upon the traveller who visited Washington

---

3. Adams, *History*, 9:221, 173.
4. Levenson, *The Mind and Art of Henry Adams*, 117–18; Adams, *Education*, 91–92.

in 1800, and mused among the unraised columns of the Capitol upon the destiny of the United States."[5]

This traveler, musing like Gibbon before the ruins of Rome, was a device to reveal Adams's design, but an actual visitor present in Washington when President John Adams addressed the first Congress to convene in the new capital would have heard Henry Adams's great-grandfather sound a more confident note. The president noted that "accommodations are not now so complete as might be wished," but he described the city as "the capital of a great nation advancing with unexampled rapidity in arts, in commerce, in wealth, and in population, and possessing within itself those energies and resources which, if not thrown away or lamentably misdirected, will secure to it a long course of prosperity and self-government."[6] President Adams's words projected a nation further on its way to achieving national identity in 1800 than Henry Adams was prepared to admit.

At the end of his introductory overview of the United States in 1800, Henry Adams also revealed more of his overall theme when he gave a hint of what was to be found at the conclusion of his large work. Here he suggested that if Americans in 1800 "were right in thinking that the next necessity of human progress was to lift the average man upon an intellectual and social level with the most favored," then Europe with all its achievements was behind America, as most Americans out of ignorance believed. Europe would be no match for the "lithe young figure" of America. "Stripped for the hardest work, every muscle firm and elastic, every ounce of brain ready for use, and not a trace of superfluous flesh on his nervous and supple body, the American," Adams wrote, "stood in the world a new order of man."[7] Devoting several pages

---

5. Adams, *History*, 1:30–31.

6. Adams, Fourth Annual Address, Nov. 22, 1800, Israel, *State of the Union Messages*, 1:52–53.

7. Adams, *History*, 1:157–60; see also Barolsky, "Henry Adams," 117–18.

to recent inventions coming from the minds of Americans mainly from humble backgrounds and with little formal education, Adams wrote that all these men were products of typical American society and "all their inventions transmuted the democratic instinct into a practical and tangible shape. Who would undertake to say," he asked, "that there was a limit to the fecundity of his teeming source?"[8] The thrust of these comments—so little in accord with most of what Adams had written about American society in 1800—was more in harmony with his summation of the United States in 1816. While this may have been added to prepare the reader for a rapidly changing country, it did little to modify the images of a backward, static society in 1800.

Despite the grand theme of the achievement of American nationality—introduced with a sweeping survey of American society in 1800 and brought to a close with an equally broad assessment of the American people in 1816—the intervening history of the presidential administrations of Jefferson and Madison offered only indirect and often subtle elaboration of the theme. The main body of the nine-volume *History* was a detailed treatment of political, diplomatic, and military history, but in occasional digressions Adams added guideposts. By recurrent references to the development of the steamboat, Adams injected a device to project progress. He hailed the voyage of Robert Fulton's *Clermont* in 1807 as being of far greater significance than the British attack on the United States frigate *Chesapeake* or Burr's conspiracy—both of which events occurred in the same year. "The problem of steam navigation, so far as it applied to rivers and harbors was settled," he proclaimed, "and for the first time America could consider herself mistress of her vast resources." Still, the narrative offered only fleeting guidance in understanding how the static society that Adams pictured in 1800 evolved into the dynamic American nation of 1816. Adams's political narrative, in fact, seemed to present a record more of decline than ascent. Jefferson emerged as a president who compromised the political

8. Adams, *History*, 1:182–83.

principles that he proclaimed in taking office and left the presidency in the wake of the foreign policy disaster of the embargo act of 1807. Adams's portrait of Madison was even less encouraging. After two years under Madison, "the government of the United States reached . . . the lowest point of its long decline," Adams wrote. Yet Adams indicated that despite Jefferson's faltering leadership, the underlying health of American society had saved the country from Burr's conspiracy; and in spite of Madison's bungling wartime leadership, the failure of the obstructionist opposition of New England Federalists to the War of 1812 provided striking evidence of the triumph of American nationalism.[9]

Adams's autobiography provides little help in understanding the writing of the *History*, which he only fleetingly mentioned. In *The Education of Henry Adams*, he skipped over the entire period during which he wrote the *History*—not because of this work but because of his wife's suicide, which came during that time. In the closing chapters of *The Education*, one can find, however, some references to the year 1800. Adams wrote of 1800 as the starting date for an accelerating rate of development that was to characterize modern times, not simply the development of the United States.[10] For formulating general laws of history, in which Adams was then much interested, this was not exceptionable. But more precision was required in describing the early history of the United States, for which the year 1800 had meaning and importance that Adams's literary artistry blurred.

Some of Adams's writings elsewhere throw light on his theme of the development of American nationality. Writing in the *North American Review* in 1876 on his view of the progress of civilization, he spoke of the "real majesty and force of the national movement" and said that "if the historian will only consent to shut his eyes for a moment to the microscopic analysis of personal

---

9. Ibid., 4:135, 5:359; Levenson, *The Mind and Art of Henry Adams*, 135–39.
10. Adams, *Education*, 485, 486, 490, 496, 497, 501.

motives and idiosyncrasies, he cannot but become conscious of a silent pulsation that commands his respect, a steady movement that resembles in its mode of operation the mechanical action of Nature herself."[11] In his history of the United States during Jefferson's and Madison's administrations, he sensed the silent pulsations of nationality overrunning all failures of faltering administrations and obstacles of localist opposition. "In 1815 for the first time Americans ceased to doubt the path they were to follow," he wrote in closing his *History*. "Not only was the unity of their nation established, but its probable divergence from older societies was also well defined." American distinction was more evident in politics than in social, religious, literary, or scientific directions, but "already by 1817 the difference between Europe and America was decided."[12]

No one can deny that the end of the War of 1812 marked a turning point, closing an earlier era of a young nation seeking to survive in a hostile world and opening up a remarkable period of American growth and expansion. But Adams's grand theme, however effective as a literary device, distorted the state of the nation in 1800 by neglecting a quarter century of great change that had begun with the American Revolution. Indeed, as one scholar has written, Adams, in the opening chapter of his *History*, "established a single character for all the past before 1800."[13]

Adams's literary artistry also obscured the importance of the year 1800 as marking, next to the adoption of the Constitution, the most critical political change since the Revolution. That change had repercussions throughout American society—bringing advances toward a more equal social order and improved opportunities to achieve the things that Adams recognized as in existence by the beginning of 1817. American society in 1800 deserves the further study that may have been discouraged by the success of Henry Adams's brilliant but flawed narrative.

---

11. Quoted in Jordy, *Henry Adams*, 74.
12. Adams, *History*, 9:220; Jordy, *Henry Adams*, 75.
13. Levenson, *The Mind and Art of Henry Adams*, 153.

✦✦✦ INDEX ✦✦✦

❖❖❖ *Index* ❖❖❖